THE GIFT OF CRISIS

FINDING YOUR BEST SELF IN THE WORST OF TIMES

I0169498

SUSAN J. MECCA PH.D.

Published by Soul Circle: Dallas, TX

Copyright © 2017, by Susan J Mecca, Ph.D.

Photography by Karen Almond Photography
Cover design by Bogdan Matei
Book design by Guido Henkel

In the years our family fought for the survival of our men, Nick and Vito taught me love always brings transformation to our lives. That love is endless and can never be taken away from us, even when we can no longer see its source.

To Nick and Vito
All my love

Table of Contents

INTRODUCTION:
THE GIFT OF CRISIS

Overnight, or in the space of the time it takes for a brief phone call or conversation, our lives become divided forever into "before" and "after." Unexpectedly or confirming our worst fears, there it is—a divorce, a life-altering diagnosis, a bankruptcy, the unexpected loss of a job, a national tragedy, or other form of life interruption or trauma. Our normal routines are unceremoniously shoved aside; our daily tasks and interactions are completely re-prioritized. An event occurs, wrenching away our illusion of control and turning our ability to navigate our lives upside down.

But what if a personal, medical, economic, or professional crisis could also be the catalyst for something positive? What if, buried in the tears, anxiety, sleepless nights, anger, and fear crises can bring, there is also the possibility of personal, psychological treasure? Would we be willing to seek out the treasure? If so, how would we find it? I have seen friends and clients emerge wiser, more successful, and more loving from disasters which felled other strong souls. What makes the difference?

Twenty years before the series of devastating medical events that occurred in the lives of my son and my husband, I had read Victor Frankl's *Man's Search for Meaning*. In this book he relates how, in the midst of the uncontrollable horrors and brutality of a Nazi concentration camp, he had uncovered the one freedom over which he could still maintain control. It was the freedom "to choose one's attitude in any given set of circumstances, to choose one's own way." It became a passion for me, in my life and in my work as both a psychologist and leadership consultant for organizations, to help my

7

clients understand and integrate this freedom in their lives. Regardless of what others said or did, in the most difficult of circumstances, they still retained the right to choose who they would be and how they would respond.

In more than thirty years working with clients as they faced tragedy or trauma, I watched them navigate their way through the experience—trying to find a way to survive the onslaught of emotions, challenges, and logistics crises bring. When my sixteen-year-old son was diagnosed with cancer, it seemed as if my entire existence had come to an abrupt standstill. Feeling out of control and helpless to change the circumstances, I turned to this belief that had become foundational in my life—I could choose who I would be during this crisis. Regardless of whether or not I had any other choices, I had this one. And from that insight, I began to find my way forward. And yet this belief was tested severely over the next three years as both my son and my husband dealt with the life-threatening illnesses altering the courses of their lives.

My clients' experiences and my own have taught me about the power of this choice. I also have come to understand that, while the energy of a crisis is invariably disruptive, it also can be transformative. I believe crises can be the Divine's way of getting our attention—a kind of crucible, melting off everything but the truest parts of ourselves. In those moments when we are jolted out of our routines or our beliefs, we can become desperate for a connection to something that feels more powerful than our individual existences. We are displaced from our normal lives. We can feel like strangers in a new land, looking carefully (and anxiously) at everything we encounter, trying to find a path to take us beyond the discomfort of this new place. And, with the disruption crises cause in our usual lives, it can also shake us loose from everything we are sure of, creating the potential for transformation.

Within crisis there is also an equal opportunity for destruction. Lives, hopes, and beliefs can be lost or altered beyond recognition. I have met with clients who, after facing a significant crisis earlier in their lives, continue to experience the world as a dark, fearsome, and angry place. They are unable to let go of the past hurt, and resentment builds, allowing the damage to persist long after the disruptive event has passed. One of my earliest areas of interest, as a psychologist, was the question of why some clients lost their way in the aftermath of a personal crisis, while others found new meaning in their lives or used the crisis as a pivot point leading them towards a more fulfilling life.

In researching the lives of people who have gone through war, hurricanes, cancer, and other life-changing events, scientists have found what they refer to as "post-traumatic growth." Tedeschi and Calhoun, early researchers of post-traumatic growth, define it as "positive psychological change that is experienced as a result of struggles with highly challenging life circumstances." Victor Frankl was one of the first to write of the counterintuitive shift he coined "tragic optimism"–looking for a way to describe the clients he saw in his therapeutic practice who had made the choice to find some benefit in the tragedies they had experienced in the Holocaust.

As someone who straddles the worlds of psychology, science, business, and metaphysics on a daily basis, I envision this "positive psychological change" as the result of a process much like gold mining. The business of prospecting is anything but glamorous – treasure seekers spend much of their lives in muddy, inhospitable terrains, exposed to the elements. Some find nothing, but others emerge with items of value and great beauty. As I watch my clients venture into the bedlam and debris of their crises in order to find nuggets of personal gold, I am awed by the psychological, spiritual, and sometimes miraculous outcomes that occur. And while not all outcomes of crises are good, I have come to believe even the worst of situations can be a catalyst for growth.

As treasure hunters have found throughout the centuries, the backbreaking process of looking for gold, real or personal, is not for everyone. The search to find meaning and growth in crisis is neither easy nor linear. Forewarned, I hope you will come on this journey of exploration. It was, for me, completely worth the process. The "Susan" who emerged (and is still emerging) from those years is far more compassionate, confident, loving, successful, and peaceful than the Susan I was when the crisis began. When I look back on those changes, forged within me by the crucible of crisis I went through, I am filled with gratitude.

Having gone through my personal crises without a manual, I hope this book will help you avoid or at least minimize the potentially destructive aspects of a crisis. My belief is, if you follow the suggestions contained within these pages, you will have a resource to help you survive the crisis, and navigate it with as much grace, resilience, and optimism as possible. With guidance, intention, and effort, I believe you can use what you've learned and how you've changed to create the potential for a positive transformation in your life. I invite you to skim the table of contents and decide what will be most useful to you, depending on where you are now. The book is arranged first by stages of a crisis and then by strategies to help you get through that period of time.

A couple of things to note about the stages. First, these stages were formulated from research and writings on transitions and change as well as the experiences of my clients and my own.[12] There are a variety of different ways to view the process. Second, stages are only roughly linear, despite how they are presented. For example, the first stage, "Survive the Initial Shock" discusses the emotional, mental, and/or physical shock most people experience when a traumatic event occurs. That being said, people will go through this process differently. For some it is an unpleasant way station they leave as quickly as possible. For others, the trauma continues to recur in their lives, rekindled by new information or events bringing back the memories of the original event.

So, I invite you to dip into the book, and skim or read the stories and the practical strategies for getting through the different stages of a crisis. Try a few ideas and decide for yourself if you find the practices or skills will be helpful to you. Or, as I like to suggest to my clients, "Read lots. Decide what makes sense to you. Toss the rest." As you read them, I hope to remind you of what you already know but have forgotten, and suggest new ways of surviving and thriving when something happens—catastrophic or simply difficult—in your life. Wherever this crisis takes you, please be assured I am sending love and prayers your way.

THE FIRST STAGE: SURVIVE THE INITIAL SHOCK

When you are going through hell, keep going.
–Winston Churchill

WHEN YOU'VE BEEN DUMPED UNCEREMONIOUSLY INTO A CRISIS, IT'S much like being thrown unexpectedly into an ocean. You sink for at least a few minutes into those dark, briny waters, disoriented and confused. Then, some instinct comes rushing in that causes you to fight your way back to the surface. For some, the impetus is the drive to survive and live or an unwillingness to give up—despite the seemingly irreparable change that has occurred. For others, a desire to protect those they love pushes them forward. Regardless of the driver, it's a nauseating and terrifying process, those first few moments or days. You panic and thrash around before you remember again how to keep your head above the waves, and to breathe.

The moment that changed my life irrevocably came as my husband and I listened to the urologist's call from surgery. The pathology report on our son Nick's biopsy was in and it confirmed the worst-case scenario—Nick had cancer. Our world came to an abrupt, stomach-lurching stop. We looked at each other for a few seconds—each stunned into a state of fear and grief too intense and private to be shared through words. In those few seconds while the world stood still in our lives, we were transformed from a reasonably normal couple (one kid, a cat, a dog, two stressful jobs, and a mostly-okay marriage) to two people barely breathing, trying to make sense of a world that had, without warning, lost its familiar landmarks.

13

My clients and friends talk about divorces, job losses, the tragedy of September 11th or indeed the financial crisis of 2008 as being some of the moments when their lives were disrupted by an event for which they had little or no warning. Regardless of how or why the event occurred, if it was personal, financial or an act of nature, most people have a similar experience—they feel disoriented, terrified, and numb—sometimes all at the same time. Since our family's crisis, I have gone back to the research on crisis to understand what was happening to us in those first few critical days after a traumatic event. In doing so, I have gained an extraordinary amount of respect for everything to be navigated and it has changed not only the way I work with clients in crisis but also how I now handled crises in my own life. To say a crisis is disruptive significantly understates the impact it makes physically, emotionally, and psychologically. In fact, I have found it is critical for my clients to understand what is going on within their bodies, what is normal and what is not, as well as for them to be able to regain a sense of control and comfort in the days that follow.

CHAPTER 1:
HANDLE WITH CARE

In times of life crisis, whether wild fires or smoldering
stress, the first thing I do is go back to basics…am I eating
right, am I getting enough sleep, am I getting some
physical and mental exercise every day?
–Edward Albert

If you are at the beginning of a crisis, it can be helpful to grasp what is going on within your body. The overview provided here is not comprehensive, so I have provided additional sources in the Resource section for those who want more detail. I hope as you read through the paragraphs below, you will find some solace in knowing what you are going through is normal, at least in the initial stage of a crisis. Through the years I have found that too many of my clients have a tendency to blame themselves for what is actually a normal physiological reaction to extreme stress. They hold themselves to an impossible standard—expecting their intelligence and competence will keep them from feeling the effects of what they are going through, while allowing them to power through a life-changing event.

So, what is going on, inside this skin that may feel like it no longer belongs to you? Our bodies, relying on the primitive evolutionary design of the limbic system (this includes the amygdala and is referred to frequently as the "lizard brain"), respond quickly and completely to stress or distress we perceive to be severe. Our neurochemistry kicks into action, flooding the brain and the body with massive amounts of neurochemical hormones (adrenaline, norepinephrine, cortisol, and epinephrine) to ready us to fight or flee—two of the three options we are programmed to follow in the face of anything the mind registers as dangerous—physically or emotionally. Physiologically, our blood pressure goes up, our pupils dilate, our senses become hypervigilant to any changes around us and our bodies shut down everything not currently needed such as digestion and cell repair. From a behavioral standpoint, someone experiencing a flight reaction to the crisis might find himself compulsively eating, sleeping too much, or walking away from a relationship of numerous years. Fight routinely manifests as lashing out—physically or verbally, responding to everyday occurrences with irritation, or creating distance from loved ones with hurtful words or sarcasm. The shock of the event can also cause us to freeze—unable to process information, make decisions, or articulate our thoughts—numb to what is going on around us. Worse yet, we are usually unaware of how the crisis is affecting us, finding others to blame for our anger or castigating ourselves for our inability to respond effectively to the challenges in front of us.

Not only do our bodies take the first "hit," the impact of those natural chemicals running through us does not dissipate quickly. It can be days or weeks before the after-effects of those initial few moments begin to fade. If the crisis continues—getting additional terrifying news, being put into situations that feel unsafe, having to continue to confront the upsetting events—the body will continue to pump those chemicals through our bodies, readying us to take action when needed. And, because we are already in a state of hypervigilance, even normal happenings can trigger those reactions, slowing our recovery from the initial situation.

It is normal to have a broad range of thoughts, emotions, psychological, and physical reactions to the crisis you are going through, especially at the outset. In many instances, people find the crisis, and the events leading up to it, playing over and over in their minds. This can be experienced as memories that keep intruding in your day-to-day activities, insomnia caused by the constant looping of terrifying thoughts, nightmares, or an over-the-top reaction to something reminding you of the crisis. Repeatedly, in those first few weeks, innocent comments from my friends or clients would be a catalyst for the horrible "what ifs" to come marauding through my mind.

Emotionally, quite a few of my clients find themselves tearful to the point of inaction or numbing out and/or avoiding anything that might remind them of the crisis. They get extremely busy, burying their anxiety in work or family, and become hyperactive in focusing on their to-do list. They put self-care at the invisible end of the to-do list and are, more times than not, completely out of contact with the emotions they are experiencing. I have watched as more than one client took on Superwoman or Superman characteristics, managing everything their families needed without asking for the help which could have lightened their loads—inevitably to their detriment.

Psychologically, a crisis can disrupt our lives in multiple ways. It can put into question our beliefs about God, ourselves, and those we love. Crises challenge our sense of self and our place in the world. Clients report feeling they are in perilous territory—betrayed by their bodies, their understanding of their world, or, sometimes, of God. Clients in crisis regularly blame themselves, become cynical, despair, or feel completely separated from any sense of community they had experienced before. Because of these factors, my clients routinely report more arguments with loved ones or feeling uncharacteristically aggressive about normal events such as being cut off in traffic.

Physically, the effect of the body chemicals slowly being released from our uncommonly stressed-out system can be experienced in various ways: as anger or irritability, startling easily, feeling nauseous, sweating, trembling, hyperventilation, and headaches, to name a few. Falling asleep or staying asleep can be difficult, as can eating. Taking care of the basics – eating, breathing, moving, staying hydrated, finding ways to relax –starts the journey back to effective action by allowing you to regain some control in a situation that can (at least initially) feel incredibly uncontrollable. For these and the reasons mentioned previously, it is important your healthcare team be aware of what you are going through so they can stand ready to assist you. I needed my amazing internist to fill a variety of needs: a listening ear, someone to provide resources, and someone to help me stay healthy so I could be there for my family.

STRATEGIES

STRATEGY #1. GET GROUNDED.

When we are in shock—facing something that seems impossible or coming to terms with a condition or event previously unthinkable in our lives, we can have a tendency to vacate our bodies and numb out, making it hard to discern what our bodies need to return to a state of balance. Our minds are so busy trying to absorb our new situation that we can lose track of time, forget to eat, or find ourselves running into things. As someone who normally finds comfort in food, I was completely uninterested in eating in the days following Nick's diagnosis. It didn't seem important, or indeed feasible, to eat while I was digesting this incomprehensible information. Breathing can feel like an unnatural act for some, with more than one client reporting becoming dizzy, unaware they were holding their breath, trying to prevent the crisis from unfolding. In addition to eating well (protein, vegetables, and good complex carbohydrates rather than sugary fixes), getting adequate sleep, and maintaining some kind of exercise program, try some of the following suggestions to get back into your body so you can do what needs to be done. Some ideas to try:

- Take your shoes off. Rub your feet back and forth on the carpet. The sensation will make you aware of your body. Then stand, and with your feet spread about shoulder-width apart, push as if you are on a rug and trying to split it in two with your feet. Hold the pose for at least one minute. The sensation of your legs pushing will also bring you back into the lower part of your body, centering you.

- Stamp your feet. Standing comfortably, alternating feet, lift each foot and place it firmly back down, feeling the impact of the ground in your legs. Do it for at least 30 seconds.

- Jog in place. The repeated impact of your feet on the ground brings blood into your legs and increases your energy flow. Try it for 30 seconds to a minute at a time. This is especially good if you don't have time to exercise as it can be done in a hospital hallway while waiting (of course, you might get some odd looks!).

- Aromatherapy. The sense of smell is evocative and powerful, as anyone can attest who has been transported back to childhood by the aroma of honeysuckle, certain foods cooking, or other scents. Because our reaction to smells is so personal, any fragrance or smell you find soothing or comforting (for example: lavender, rose, jasmine, lemon or peppermint) will have a positive influence on your mental or emotional state. Beyond personal preference, skilled aromatherapists have discovered a class of essential oils called sesquiterpenes impact the nervous system, soothing it when you have been stressed. Oils falling into this category include cedarwood, spikenard, vetiver, sandalwood, and patchouli. The quality of the essential oil is extremely important, so do your research and buy from someone who carefully sources their oils. These oils need a carrier oil, such as sweet almond or hazelnut oil, to facilitate their absorption into the system and should be put on the wrists and behind the knees for the best effect.[3]

- Get a massage. Massage helps you be present in your body and it provides the nurturing you may be missing. Concentrate on any feelings arising while you're on the massage table. Let them come up and flow out of you as your muscles relax. Pay attention to the parts of you holding onto the tension so you can release those muscles more consciously. For example, I consistently find my clients carry tension in the upper back region. Remembering to simply drop the shoulders from time to time will help alleviate the soreness. In addition, you may want to ask if your massage therapist can include some aromatherapy (see above for suggestions) for stress relief and grounding.

- Yoga postures. Hatha yoga, in particular, has several postures that support grounding. Consider dropping in on a local yoga class to determine if it helps you handle the stress of the crisis.

STRATEGY #2. RECOGNIZE THE FEAR.

The impact of fear is multi-faceted—emotional, physical, and mental. With fear in the foreground, we can feel cut off from the positive emotions available to us—the love of family, the embrace of the Divine, the caring of friends—making the fear feel isolating and inescapable. Physically, fear can feel like a rock in the pit of your stomach, a tightening across your chest, a feeling of nerves running through your body, or an ache in your shoulders. Regardless of how you are experiencing the fear, it typically seems overwhelming.

Because the purpose of our limbic system is to strengthen us when we encounter something we deem to be dangerous, it immediately takes over. Our heart pounds, we feel faint, and we sweat. Urgently our old lizard brain sends us messages to fight, freeze, or run like hell away from the danger. With the screaming going on from our limbic system, our frontal lobe – the place of reason, analytical thinking, and judgment – is pushed to the background. As Jon Kabat-Zinn points out in his classic, *Full Catastrophe Living: Using the Wisdom of Your Body and Mind to Face Stress, Pain, and Illness*, fear can lead to a feeling you've lost control over your life and to panic. These reactions are completely counter to what is actually needed from you at that time—the ability to respond to the immediate crisis with thoughtful analysis and decision-making. Recognize the sensations you are experiencing are natural and related to the fear. Rather than trying to fix it or make it go away, merely observe it. Research suggests that labeling an emotion calms the response in our amygdala.[4] This was a huge insight for Steven, a young man in his thirties. Steven can easily spiral into a fairly dark place when work and family stress seem overwhelming. He discovered when he simply watched the negative emotions rise up within him, and labeled them as fear, guilt, or shame without trying to figure out why he was feeling that way, he was able to stay out of the grim thoughts more successfully.

STRATEGY #3. BREATHE.

One of the most immediate and simple ways to get your brain to calm down, and begin to operate more strategically, is to focus on your breathing—something you *can* control. While most of my clients understand their breathing is important, I'm continually surprised by the number of them who (like me) unconsciously hold their breath when anxious. They forget the importance of deep breathing in helping the body return to a calmer, less alert status. When frightening or sudden events occur, the body automatically begins to breathe quickly and shallowly as part of its survival instinct. Continuing to breathe shallowly will prolong the heightened sense of stimulation, preventing you from calming down and taking more intentional action.

Take a few moments to notice how you are breathing. Are you holding your breath? Breathing rapidly? Or are you supporting your body with slow, deep, regular breaths? Because breathing is such an important and basic way to re-center yourself for effective action, it is helpful to look at some ways to use your breath to do so.

- Diaphragmatic breathing. This exercise is particularly useful when you feel as if anxiety or stress is about to overwhelm you.

    - *Step one*: Sit up straight. The tendency is to hunch over when dealing with something impacting you like a body blow. When you're in a fetal position, it's impossible to breathe deeply. Be aware of your posture while you breathe.

o *Step two*: Put one hand on your stomach and the other on your chest.

o *Step three*: Slowly breathe in through your nose, making sure the hand on your stomach moves as the breath you take expands it. Watch to make sure the hand on your chest stays still.

o *Step four*: Blow out your breath slowly through your mouth.

o Repeat at least 5-10 times.

If you begin to feel lightheaded (as did one of my clients, before I learned to add the part about breathing *slowly*), you are probably breathing too shallowly or quickly and may be hyperventilating. Slow down so the inward breath takes at least five seconds and the outward breath takes as long or longer. The deep breathing should alleviate the heart pounding and lightheadedness. If not, immediately consult a physician (if you haven't already).

• Breathe in beauty—A technique I love and teach my clients is to "breathe in beauty." This is a process that integrates breathing with a form of imagery and can be done anywhere you see something beautiful—a picture, a vase of flowers, the face of a child, a tree. I like to do it when walking out of doors, bringing activity to the practice, something research[5] has shown to be useful.

If you choose to do this exercise while you walk, you will want to be watching for sights you find to be peaceful, relaxing, or beautiful. In the summertime in Dallas, crepe myrtle trees are in bloom and they are everywhere in my older neighborhood. Their vibrant pink, red, and white blossoms provide a constant source of beauty for me. As you walk, keep your pace steady enough to support slow, deep breathing. Then, find something beautiful in front of you. Breathing in, imagine you are pulling the vision into your lungs. Observe the colors, scents, textures, and shapes of it flowing into your body, flooding you with the experience it invokes in you. When you breathe out, feel the stress, anxiety, worry, and fear leave your body and disappear into the light. When you pass it by, quickly focus your eyes on the next spot you find beautiful. Repeat five to ten times or throughout your entire walk. If you choose to do this while seated, bring what you are choosing to focus on close enough in order to perceive it clearly. Using the same slow, steady, in-and-out breaths, breathe in the beauty and breathe out the stress. Repeat the exercise as regularly as possible.

STRATEGY #4. FIND A SAFE PLACE TO CRY.

The initial stages of a crisis can bring seemingly unlimited tears and those of us who are criers by nature have experienced the release a good cry can bring. Uninterrupted time to let the tears flow naturally can clear the mind and bring a sense of calm. If you find yourself crying frequently in the days immediately after a crisis, give some thought to creating a time and place for those tears. Some people use the car, the shower, walks with their dog, church, or their bedroom. Regardless of where you choose, after you are done crying, create some kind of ritual to indicate to yourself you have finished. It can be as simple and natural as washing your face or it can be a healing moment of meditation where you send love to the person or the situation. Other ways to "finish" could be:

- Say a prayer.

- Use a mantra that resonates for you.

- State an affirmation such as "I let this go and let this loose" or "I release this situation to God for healing."

- Take a shower.

STRATEGY #5. STAY WARM.

Hospitals and clinics can be harsh places to wait, especially when you're in the initial stages of a medically related shock. Take care of your practical needs in a way that is as soothing and nurturing as possible. Stock a big tote or backpack with bottled water, something warm (clothing or liquid), change for the vending machines, and something to read. Add things you need or will make you feel comfortable—antacids, scented lotion, essential oils, socks for cold feet. Take it with you every time you go, even if you have every reason to assume it will be a brief appointment. If you are not required to be in a hospital or clinic, you can nurture yourself in similar ways, at home or in your office. One client, going through an extremely stressful time in her career, stocked up on her favorite teas and snacks as a way to take care of herself at work. Others have brought in comforting music, flowers, or earphones, which allow them to tune out the noises that can be extremely jangling when your nervous system is on high alert.

I don't know whether it was fear, exhaustion, or a lowered immune system due to shock, but I was perpetually freezing whenever we sat in the waiting room of the oncology clinic. After several occasions when I had to ask for blankets to keep my teeth from chattering, I decided to find a throw to bring with me. I chose a purple, soft, chenille throw as a way to nurture my spirit (purple is associated with spiritual connection), appeal to my tactile senses that wanted something comforting, and keep me warm.

As simple as it seems, taking care of the basics is the first step towards regaining your balance during the first part of a crisis. Equally important is to remember that, in your current state, your brain may not be functioning at its capacity. Spending a few moments to breathe, ground, and nurture yourself will pay off by getting you back on track more quickly.

CHAPTER 2:
TAKE IT SLOW

I am always wary of decisions made hastily. I am always wary of the first decision, that is, the first thing that comes to my mind if I have to make a decision. This is usually the wrong thing. I have to wait and assess, looking deep into myself, taking the necessary time.
–Pope Francis

Crises can unfold at the speed of light, making it feel critical to move as quickly as possible to respond to what emerges. I believe we react that way for various reasons: the lizard brain at work, trying to move us quickly from what appears to be a dangerous situation; the desire for action and problem-solving ingrained within some of us; or a sense of urgency we can experience because of the suddenness of the crisis.

If you view a crisis being similar to driving on an icy road, this idea of proceeding carefully and thoughtfully makes sense. While the desire may be intense to get beyond the icy patches and get home safely, our chances of doing so are significantly increased when we stay cautious and alert to those around us, to road conditions, and to the reactions of our cars. So unless the situation is truly life-threatening, take a few moments, ask some important questions, and refuse to give into the panicky belief we have to act rapidly. You may save yourself from later regret.

STRATEGIES

STRATEGY #1. APPROACH DECISIONS THOUGHT-FULLY.

In the initial stages of a crisis we can be asked to make critical decisions quickly. Recognize that, when reeling from the initial shock, you may not be thinking clearly. Decision-making literature[6] suggests that, under stress, two tendencies can lead to poor decision making. First is the inclination, when feeling pressure-prompted, to miss some of the important alternatives when deciding which path to take. When you are trying to make a decision quickly, it makes sense that you may not consider or understand all of the available options. The second issue is a human propensity, particularly under stress, to seek reward rather than punishment. In decision-making, this can lead you to overemphasize the potential of positive outcomes and miss the possibility of negative ones. To help you make better decisions while your brain, body, and emotions are in a swirl, consider pulling in some expert resources such as a professional, friend, or family member to help you sort through the decisions you are facing. Questions to consider:

- Which decisions must be made now? Is it a preference, a suggestion, or a necessity to act immediately?

- What are the consequences of putting off the decision for 24-48 hours? Try to keep your anxiety from driving you to a premature conclusion.

- If the decision must be made immediately, what are the pros and cons of each option?

- How can I get a second opinion and who can help me obtain it quickly?

STRATEGY #2. TAKE TIME OUT.

The stereotype of the British is that, when faced with momentous decisions, they make tea. There is something quite wise about doing so. When our limbic system is engaged, our frontal lobe is running a distant second in decision-making. The part of us that has been hardwired to react to perceived threats in the environment has, in all likelihood, taken over the process of determining appropriate next steps. Taking time out to brew and drink a cup of tea allows the limbic system time to subside and the frontal lobe to step forward. Regardless if you like tea or not, take the equivalent time (at least twenty minutes) to allow the adrenaline to settle down before you make a decision (if possible). Other ways to allow time for your frontal lobe to get back in charge of the decision could be to:

- Pick up a book and read for a half-hour. If you enjoy reading (and I love it, which is why I put this first), spending twenty minutes with an engaging book can transport you to another place, where the crisis may not follow. Set the timer for twenty minutes. At the end of that time, you will be better able to approach your choices with less adrenaline running through your body and triggering your fears.

- Go for a twenty-minute walk. Getting outside both changes the scenery and works off some of the adrenaline.

- Talk to someone soothing about what is going on. But don't pick someone who will trigger or match your fears. You'll wind yourself up further.

- Write out your thoughts. In order to express yourself, language is required, something our old lizard brains (where the fear and anxiety reactions are occurring) do not have. For more on the impact of expressive writing and anxiety reduction, see Stage 4, Chapter 1, "Strategy #2: Write your path forward".

STRATEGY #3. LIMIT WHAT YOU TAKE ON.

There is a reason you may be feeling overwhelmed in these initial days of the crisis—you are being flooded with new information, fluctuating emotions, disturbing physical sensations, racing thoughts, and a hundred other unfamiliar stimuli. In the midst of this whirlwind, sometimes the smartest thing you can do is to say "no"— to yourself and to others. While you are finding your way back to the surface, it is not the time to go on a diet, catch up on overdue tasks, redecorate your house, take on a huge project at work or home, or chair a committee. As a wise therapist once told me early in my career when I was whining about my inability to lose weight at the same time I was struggling with a snarky, demanding boss, a long-distance relationship, and job burnout, "You can only do so much, Susan." And yet, somehow, we believe we have to maintain our current crazy lives despite the fact our world may have gone completely out of its usual orbit. A friend of mine, shortly after being diagnosed with breast cancer, was offered a promotion…and took it! Somehow, saying, "No, I have a serious disease and need to take care of myself" didn't seem like an option to her. The reality is, most people will graciously understand your need to say no. If they don't, their response will tell you more about who they are than who you are. Two ways to prioritize what you take on include:

- Be honest with yourself—is it a necessity or a strong prefer-ence? How truly important is this task?

- Another boss of mine (not the snarky one) honed his to-do list by using simple criteria to prioritize tasks. At the top were the most critical tasks – things that would cost him his job if he failed to complete them. From there he considered whom he would anger if he were to neglect their requests, how badly they would react to the neglect, and how important the person was to his career. His point was—everything is urgent to someone. He was ultimately responsible for deciding what was most important to him.

Regardless of the system you use to make your decisions about what needs to be done, stay intentional rather than reacting to the urgency of others or your desire to feel productive. You have limited energy in the midst of a crisis. Use it wisely!

STRATEGY #4. FOCUS ON THE FAMILIAR.

When Nick was released from post-op into a recovery room, he was groggy and in some pain. As we waited for the pain medications to take effect, I did the only thing I knew to do to nurture Nick—Reiki —a form of energy healing. I'd had only one class in Reiki, but knew enough of the theory behind the methods of shepherding the pain away from the body, releasing it, to try it on Nick. Slowly, intent on bringing him some measure of relief, I visualized the pain moving down his body and away from him, following the movement of my hands. After a few moments, Nick opened his eyes and watched what I was doing. "Mom," he said, "this is probably not the best time for people to find out just how weird you are." This tsunami had flooded our lives, but some of the old landmarks were still visible. I could still embarrass our adolescent son with my metaphysical "weirdness."

While you are still trying to reorient yourself to the new conditions you are facing, identify what is good and consistent in your life. While everything else around you is in flux, these can become your anchors. To identify your personal anchors:

- Make a list of the things you are sure you can still count on, especially during the crisis. Identifying them will help you recognize that some part of your old life remains. Oft times, when we go through a crisis, it feels as if everything has changed and there is nothing of our old life.

- When you begin to feel overwhelmed by the changes surrounding you, take a moment to remember those landmarks. Find a way to integrate them into your life on a regular basis. For one client whose husband had been diagnosed with cancer, maintaining the family dinner hour (whenever possible) helped her create a sense of normalcy for her young sons.

When you are focusing on the familiar, taking things slowly at first makes sense. If you've ever had the wind knocked out of you, you remember both the panic and the time it took to recapture your breath. And, once you did, I suspect that you did not immediately take off at a run. You possibly spent a little time reassuring yourself you were once again breathing, and perhaps moved tentatively before resuming your normal pace. Give yourself some time to adjust before moving on. And, when getting back on your feet, it can be useful to have someone you trust there to spot you.

CHAPTER 3:
GET HELP

*We all want to help one another. Human beings
are like that.*
–Charlie Chaplin

One of the first things that customarily happens when an earth-quake, tornado, or flood hits a community is a call for volunteers. It is a lovely aspect of our humanness that such a large number of us want to offer a helping hand when tragedies or disasters occur in the lives of others. Following the tragedy of September 11, 2001, there were countless stories of strangers reaching out to comfort and lend a hand to those whose lives had been devastated by the attack. But a disaster is not the only reason we reach out to help one another. It has been my experience, and that of my clients, that there are a sub-stantial number of compassionate souls around who are willing to guide us to stable ground. However, to get the assistance we must first recognize the fears and beliefs which can prevent us from doing so.

My clients who struggle most with the idea of requesting help from others, when a crisis hits their lives, are frequently the highly com-petent ones who excel at problem solving. While they are regularly called upon by others to offer solutions or practical assistance, it can be difficult for them to invite the same into their lives. One client, an exceptionally capable technical manager, working two nigh-impossible jobs at the same time—caring for his wife with cancer and managing a widely dispersed team through the thorny imple-mentation of a new product design—faced this problem. Letting go of his belief he should be able to handle anything that came his way—a quality contributing greatly to his career success—was the first difficult step. Starting with small, easily manageable requests of family and friends, he was surprised and overwhelmed with gratitude by their immediate, and competent, responses.

STRATEGIES

STRATEGY #1: FIND A LIFELINE.

During my training as a psychologist, I, like some of my colleagues, spent a summer of weekend nights in the psychiatric emergency room of a local hospital. We did crisis assessment, intervention, and stabilization those hot Dallas nights from five until midnight. After determining the patient was safe and no longer in medical crisis, we took extensive medical, social, and psychological histories from the patients and their families. In those long conversations, we were looking for, at least in part, someone who would support the patients in their time of need. As medical professionals we knew the research on the impact this could have. For example, studies following breast cancer patients have shown that having emotional support has been predictive of less depression,[7] shorter hospital stays,[8] and a greater likelihood of experiencing personal growth after breast cancer.[9] In general, over the last twenty years, research has found that having emotional support during stress helps both our psychological and physical health.[10]

For some people, the automatic reaction to a bone-jarring shock or fearsome event is to retreat or hunker down alone. While this is a normal initial response, research tells us people who isolate during a crisis can experience significantly worse outcomes than those who have a community to draw on.[11] Resist the urge to handle the crisis by yourself. It is reasonable to assume you will not be operating optimally during the early days of your crisis. Pull people into your life who will provide the support you need, both during the initial shock and down the road, once you are clearer about the kind of help you will need to handle the crisis effectively.

In this initial stage it is important, before you reach out, to analyze what you need _right now_. Is it someone to take charge or simply listen? Do you need a soft place to land or someone who will help you start to plan? Pick the person who will give you what you need. Don't feel obligated to tell everyone what is going on.

My client, Rick, was in the launching stage of his cutting-edge technology company. He was completely focused on his business, usually to the exclusion of his personal life. When Rick was diagnosed with testicular cancer at age thirty-four, his first act (ignoring the fact his girlfriend was sitting in the waiting room) was to text his partner, "Bad news. It's cancer. May have to miss a few days." He needed to inform his friend and partner he might not be completely available at this critical time (he actually only missed four days during the entire six-month protocol). Rick told the rest of his family the news slowly, matching the information flow to his need to stay focused on what was still the most important thing in his life—his business. While Rick's level of single-mindedness may not resonate with you, consider the broader lesson. It's okay to take care of yourself and to be thoughtful about whom you invite into your crisis.

If you don't have supportive family or friends, or if it feels uncomfortable to share the news with them, consider finding a coach, therapist, minister, or other helping professional to assist you through the crisis. Frequently, my clients come to therapy during a crisis because of the physical or psychological distance they feel from their families. Adelina was eighteen and had recently miscarried her baby when she came into therapy with me. Because she was pregnant out of wedlock, her family saw the miscarriage as a blessing and were impatient with her grief process. Adelina needed a supportive place to process the intense feelings she was experiencing before she could begin to decide what she would do next.

As you decide who to contact during the initial days of this crisis, some questions to consider might be:

- Who will bring a positive attitude and thoughtfulness into my life through their presence, actions, or words?

- Who might be a source of good judgment or wisdom?

- Who knows me, values me, and sees the best in me?

- Who has the compassion and the thoughtful honesty to help me stay on track?

- Who will bring their best selves (consistently) to our interactions?

When we answer the questions above, we may naturally focus on whose responses are relatively predictable. As a rule, they are the first people we consider, particularly if our experience of their support is positive, loving, and helpful. Because we know them, we can be intentional about whom we contact and what we ask for. We are aware of who has the job that makes it easiest to get time off and come to our assistance. We recognize who will be able to be in the room for the hard news, keep his or her head, ask good questions, and stay clear when we might be muddled. We have also learned, through experience, who is liable to need our support more than give us theirs or whose reactions will drain us at a time when we are running on empty. We can distinguish who will say, "yes" and who will say, "gosh, I would love to but this is a bad time for me."

It is also important to recognize your needs may change as the timeline of the crisis unfolds. Those "first responders" in your crisis generally will be those who are most accessible or available at the time your life is first turned upside down. Their purpose may only be to help you through the initial shock and, having done so beautifully, may disappear or become less available. You, too, will grasp more about what you need from your support system as time goes on. This first step of reaching out is about finding the people who will steady you on your feet when the impact of the crisis can be the most disorienting. When you are ready to move forward, a more thoughtful, less reactive approach to building a community of support will make sense *(for more about enlisting a broader range of support once you are through the initial stage of the crisis see:* **Create a Community of Support, The Third Stage, Chapter 2**).

STRATEGY #2. GET QUIET.

While the help I needed to process the fear and pain I was feeling was the support of others, my highly introverted husband needed solitude and quiet to wrap his thoughts around this radical change in our lives. As both psychologist and wife, I had come to understand introverts, as a rule, must thoroughly examine and digest information before they are ready to move forward. We each had to come to terms with Nick's diagnosis in our own way. The same, I have found, is true for my clients and friends as they have dealt with unexpected and upsetting outcomes in their lives, whether the crisis is personal or caused by an external economic or political change. Some will find comfort in community and sharing while others will need quiet reflection time to come to grips with the event.

If you need solitude and space to come to grips with this change, tell those around you. Most people will try to help you in the way they would want to be helped, regardless of how well their preferences would work for you. They will be grateful for any kind of instructions from you. If your need for solitude is not respected (and sometimes others' anxiety gets in the way of leaving you alone), find ways to claim it. Go for a walk, retire early for the evening, turn off your cell phone, go for a run, close your eyes and pretend to be asleep—whatever will allow you the time away you need.

As you go through these initial days of crisis, honor your inner wisdom about what you need and when you need it. If it feels difficult or hard to do so, consider asking someone else to be your advocate, or use other means of communication, such as email, to let people in on how they can best help you.

STRATEGY #3. TALK ABOUT IT.

Recently a dear friend lost her battle with depression and killed herself. Her husband found the body and was traumatized by the violence of the scene. In the hours following the suicide, I received several phone calls from concerned loved ones, trying to help the husband. My advice was simple: "Let him talk about it." He had experienced a horrible, terrifying event and his brain was trying to make sense of it. Talking out loud, sometimes repetitively, about something shocking to us is a natural way to process what has happened. Sometimes, family members will encourage the person to keep quiet—out of a mistaken belief that dwelling on a horrible event causes more pain, or because they don't want to hear the information themselves. When we process anxiety-provoking information in our heads, we have a tendency to continue spinning. Yet when we begin to label what we are feeling we begin to calm down our lizard brain, allowing our frontal lobe to begin to take back control. If you are able to verbalize what you've seen or are feeling, consider finding someone who will listen supportively, without trying to move you too quickly into problem-solving. If there is no one in your life or no one who is available, take out a piece of paper (or get out your computer) and write down everything rolling around in your head. You may find yourself much calmer and more focused as a result.

STRATEGY #4. DON'T FORCE YOUR PROCESS.

Despite what is written in the previous paragraph, talking about it may not be the right answer for you, to help you through the initial shock. In the research on horrific experiences (natural disasters, war, crime, for example) researchers have found these events are stored in the oldest part of our brain—the part that evolved before the language and thinking centers came into being.[12] This can make it difficult and sometime counterproductive to speak about the trauma. If you can't find the words, or if talking about what you witnessed triggers more anxiety, don't pressure yourself (or let others pressure you) to talk about it.

It is not uncommon, especially with the kinds of crises mentioned above, for people to continue to experience the symptoms discussed in this stage, long after the initial shock occurs. I would urge you, however, to consult a trained medical or mental health professional if any of the following continues to occur several weeks later:

- avoiding sights or thoughts reminding you of the crisis

- inability to process the event in any way

- hypervigilance about or overreacting to normal sounds

- inability to sleep or control negativity

- self-blaming

- self-medicating with drugs or alcohol

- experiencing persistent psychological symptoms such as an inability to concentrate, enjoy life, or move forward

- or any of the other physiological, physical, emotional, or mental reactions discussed here.

It is not a weakness to let others help you through dark times. It a strength to recognize when to reach out.

In the first few hours or days after a crisis occurs, every aspect of who you consider yourself to be can be intensely challenged. You've been thrown into deep and possibly terrifying waters. And, as with divers who find themselves briefly disoriented in the sea, it is critical to determine which way will lead you to the surface so you can begin to find your way back to safety. Experienced swimmers have learned to follow the bubbles of their breath in order to find their way to the surface. Pick one, or two, or three of the suggestions and ideas outlined in this stage and put them into practice. As you do so, remember to pay attention to your body. You will need to count on it once you reach the surface. Don't try to do too much; save your energy for the exertion ahead of you. And stretch out for those helping hands reaching towards you. May they be numerous along the way.

THE SECOND STAGE: REGAIN YOUR BALANCE

Although the road is never ending
take a step and keep walking,
do not look fearfully into the distance…
On this path let the heart be your guide
for the body is hesitant and full of fear.
–Rumi

Trying to regain your balance, sense of control, and direction in the middle of a crisis is very similar to trying to cross a fast-moving river on a narrow log. As you're inching across on an unstable piece of wood—your only separation from freezing water—it's easy to panic if something causes the log to shake. When this happens, the human tendency is to focus anxiously on the space where one's feet are and on what is creating the instability. Some people freeze in place with fearful thoughts of making the wrong move and falling running through into their minds. Others flail about fearfully and overcorrect to compensate for the shifting. Those actions are typically rewarded with an icy dunk in the river water below.

The better bet is to stay flexible and still, breathing deeply. Take a minute to look around and relax. Chances are there is beauty around you. Enjoy it, if only for a minute. Laugh, if you can, at the absurdity of the situation and everything you are doing to stay upright. Notice what is happening around you, gathering any new information you may need to help you make it across the river.

When you are ready, reorient yourself and focus on where you are trying to go, using the other side of the river as your end point. By being mindful of where you are—focusing on your goal and not your fears, letting other thoughts drop away, and gripping the surface firmly beneath you with your toes—you can begin to inch steadily in the direction of your objective. Calm and focused, you have a better chance of both staying upright and making it to the other side warm and dry.

The illusory nature of control I had held onto for years came crashing to a halt for me the day Nick was diagnosed. Up until that point, I had done a spectacular job (or so I thought) directing the Universe with regard to Nick's medical situation. The cancer diagnosis didn't listen to my plan. I couldn't control the outcome of Nick's biopsy, no matter how much positive energy I directed that way. I'm profoundly aware now the outcome was never up to me.

I still believe positive thinking, intention, and prayer (or "distant intentionality" as scientists like to call it) work. I no longer assume I can control any outcomes with them. Outcomes, I've come to accept, dance to a distant and more complex set of variables than human will.

When I gave up trying to control the Universe (which, admittedly, I was pretty lousy at), I discovered something important I could control—myself. I had total and complete control over how I responded to the crisis, the attitude and expectations I came with, the way I treated others and myself—those variables were within my control.

I have begun to understand how much our desire to control the events of our lives comes from an erroneous belief that permanent balance can be achieved and maintained in our lives. It's an illusion, brought to us by the popular media and our own perpetually chattering thoughts. The reality is our lives are more like airplanes than anything else. In flight, airplanes are more frequently off the flight plan than on it. Pilots spend their flight time constantly responding to shifts in air currents, weather conditions, and other disruptions to the flight path. So do we spend our lives getting out of balance and then finding ways to regain it. Balance is not a steady state one can achieve and sustain; it's an ongoing process in our lives.

While pilots can utilize the flight plan they are given to continuously adjust their course across the sky, we can use the power of intentionality to steer ourselves. Setting a goal for our behavior and our attitude during the crisis is the first step in the process of finding some measure of balance. We can then correct our course, using those intentions, when the disruptions of racing or negative mind noise and fearful, obsessive thoughts challenge our equilibrium.

CHAPTER 1:
DEFINE YOUR INTENT

You can't cross a sea by merely staring into the water.
–Rabindranath Tagore

Crises create huge shifts in the patterns of our lives and, like severe turbulence, can require significant time and readjustment before we get our lives back on a more even keel. In order to regain our balance, it is helpful to have a focal point, a purpose or direction, which doesn't shift regardless of the changing circumstances surrounding us. Unlike the concept of creating change in our lives by setting a clear intention to have something or achieve a particular goal and then releasing it, trusting the Universe will bring it to you (Wayne Dyer writes beautifully about this in his book, *The Power of Intention*), intentionality means being both goal-oriented and thoughtful in your actions, rather than reactive.

I have spoken on the subject of intentionality to the leaders with whom I had the opportunity to work for close to twenty years. In coaching sessions and training workshops across the globe, I talked about being conscious, reflective, and intentional in our interactions with others. When the leaders I worked with needed to navigate the frequently stressful, tense, or murky waters of their business and personal lives, I coached them to answer first the question, "Who do I want to be in this situation?" And I have found, once this key goal has been named, it gives us a place to begin—to convert the intention into behaviors and actions. For example, Jack—a leader whose intention was to be transparent during a company crisis—recognized how important it was to communicate not only his decisions but the rationale and data which had led to the conclusion. Claire, an entrepreneur responding to a business downturn, wanted to be more strategic in her actions. Focusing on this intent allowed her to recognize that staying mired in the minutiae of her direct reports' responsibilities detracted from her goal.

Deciding who you want to be, how you want to get through crisis, the qualities and characteristics you want to demonstrate, or the values you want to embody are ways to create your focal point or "flight path." With those clearly stated, you can recognize when you are off-course, adjust your actions or attitudes, and move back into the way of being most congruent with your intent.

Early in my therapeutic work with Chris, a young man coming to terms with the fact that his marriage was unexpectedly ending, I asked, *"Who do you believe your children need you to be, in order to stay as whole as possible?"* Despite his raging anger at his wife's affair, which had led to the dissolution of their marriage, Chris wanted his sons to hear from him it was okay to still love their mother. This was his stated goal. To prevent them from feeling as if they had to be angry at their mother on his behalf, he decided he wanted to speak about his wife (in the presence of his children at least!) in a positive, non-blaming way. This was despite his very human desire to point out to them, in living color, his spouse's personal flaws and misdeeds. As we continued to work together, he articulated how incredibly difficult it had been, especially at the beginning, to suppress the sarcastic and defensive thoughts which frequently arose when, for example, his wife would cancel plans with their sons at the last moment because it was inconvenient for her. Yet Chris believed his sons were more comfortable expressing their hurt and sadness when their mom didn't show up, because they did not have to defend her actions to their father.

With Nick's diagnosis, I had come face to face with my inability to control the Universe. That message was reinforced, on steroids, when seven months after Nick started chemotherapy, my beloved, strong, and competent husband, Vito, contracted Guillain-Barré. This devastating neurological disease took him from being a healthy runner to being completely paralyzed from the neck down, forced to rely on a respirator and feeding tube to survive. With this new crisis, I had the option of staying in a state of extreme anxiety or following my own counsel. I call these "put up or shut up" moments. These are the times when you're faced with the opportunity to live out the sermons you've been preaching to others. I personally find the "put up or shut up" moments to initially be irritating but, ultimately, illuminating when they occur in my life.

I found having a goal in mind about who I wanted to be gave me something positive and actionable to focus on, when so much seemed out of my control. Asking myself the same questions I had, for years, asked others brought forth an answer that seemed curiously satisfying and grounding. My intentions were to stay present, to do everything in my power to ensure our family emerged from these illnesses physically, emotionally, and psychologically whole, to stay healthy myself, and to be the person my men needed me to be. I knew how I approached this next crisis and the ways in which I chose to interact with others were fully in my control, regardless of whether or not anything else was.

STRATEGIES

STRATEGY #1. STOP, TURN INWARD, AND REFLECT.

Creating intentionality is not something to be done on the fly. Find some space within the craziness of your day to start this process.

- *Step one*: Get comfortable in a chair and sit in silence or with soothing music in the background, if only for five minutes.

- *Step two*: Breathe deeply; let the stresses of the day start to dissipate. Imagine them flowing out of your body (see the deep breathing exercise in the previous section).

- *Step three*: Roll your neck, stretch, and rub your feet against the floor to get grounded and back in your body. Most of us, particularly in crisis mode, spend the day in our heads, ignoring our bodies.

For your deepest wisdom to emerge about who you want to be and how you want to act, you have to be available to listen to what your soul is telling you. For a few slow, deep breaths, allow the racing thoughts and worries of the day to fade—breathe in the quiet and breathe out the thoughts as they arise. Then, read the following reflections and jot your answers down on a piece of paper.

- *Step four*: Imagine it is six months after the crisis has passed. Your best friend is talking to you about what s/he admired most about you during the crisis. What do you hope s/he will tell you?

- *Step five*: Reflect on someone (real or fictional) who has gone through severely challenging times in his or her life. What are the qualities or traits that person demonstrated through his or her personal crisis? Consider Mother Teresa and her compassion and steadfastness, for example, or the character in Rocky, for his perseverance and courage.

STRATEGY #2. SYNTHESIZE, SELECT, AND CLAIM.

Look for words that show up frequently in your answers to the questions above. Do key themes or phrases emerge from your answers to each of these questions? Write those down. When I ask my clients to do this exercise, I regularly hear responses such as "honest," "compassionate," "courageous," "optimistic," or "inspirational." People instinctively appear to want to claim the best of themselves or those qualities they most admire, despite everything else seeming upside-down.

From those themes, pick no more than three and write a brief, declarative statement using each word. For example, "I face each day with courage and grace." Say the words out loud. Repeat the phrase each morning, looking at yourself in the mirror. Write, sing, yell, or dance your intentions daily until they become part of you. Find images or objects to help you remember who you are choosing to be and how you are choosing to act. For some of my clients, tying their intentions to a daily act is a great way to remember their goals. Lee, a newly single mom, worked with me to set firm and loving boundaries with her children. Each morning as she put on her jewelry she would repeat her intentions: "I am clear and steadfast in the requests I make of my children. I lovingly and calmly provide logical consequences when they choose to disobey."

STRATEGY #3. PRACTICE.

Brainstorm (with a friend, if you like) typical situations you will be facing during this crisis. Describe how you will act in those situations, demonstrating the quality or characteristic you have selected for one of your guiding stars, but stating your intent as if it is already part of who you are and what you do. This allows you to retrain your brain and begin to visualize these qualities as already in existence. For example: "When meeting with my divorce attorney to talk about my divorce, I demonstrate courage by staying calm and grounded, by asking every terrifying question I can imagine, and by admitting I am afraid." Or: "When talking to my boss about my upsetting performance review, I speak my truth by clearly stating the information I believe is inaccurate. I demonstrate poise, remaining open and curious about her perspective, asking clarifying questions when I don't understand."

If you truly want to feel competent in the conversation or situation coming up, use the trick hundreds of organizational coaching clients have learned—pick someone you trust and do a skill practice. Skill practices are a way of actually trying out, in a safe environment, the words and strategies you want to use. Ask your friend or trusted colleague to play the role of the individual you are going to engage in conversation. If they haven't met the person, explain enough about the personality traits and reactions you expect the person will demonstrate. Make an agreement that you can stop the skill practice at any time, get feedback on how it's going, or change course. The idea is not to do it perfectly the first time. It's to try out the skills sufficiently enough to feel ready to have the conversation on your own. Ask your skill practice partner to give honest but helpful feedback, providing suggestions as well as thoughtful critiques. Tell your partner the characteristics and traits you want to demonstrate in the upcoming situation so she or he can provide feedback about how well your intentions shine through.

I have done this technique hundreds of times in the twenty-five years I have been coaching senior executives. It feels uncomfortable for them at first—vulnerability is not typically encouraged in corporate America—but invariably, they cite it as one of the most useful parts of our work together. It is critical you pick someone to practice with who believes in you and wants you to be successful.

STRATEGY #4. STAY CONSCIOUS.

This is doubtless the hardest part of intentionality—staying aware of how you are operating and whether or not your actions are in alignment with your intentions. Some ideas to help you do so:

- Plan your day—Whenever possible, mentally travel through your day and the challenges you will face. Identify the ones most apt to trigger your old lizard brain and hijack your intentions through fearful thoughts and adrenaline-based reactions. Once your fight, flight, or freeze reactions have been triggered, it can be hard to stay intentional. I coach my clients to get ready for a meeting they anticipate will be difficult by writing a few words of reminder on the tops of their notepads. One of them, a senior executive who reported feeling overcome by the tension in the room caused by impending layoffs and unable to speak up, would write down both the behaviors he wanted to demonstrate—straightforward, open to others' ideas, a good listener—and the key points he wanted to make. That way, when he found himself shutting down, he had a pathway back to the outcomes he wanted to achieve in the meeting.

- Enlist an intentionality coach—Consider an intentionality coach who will help you stay deliberate in your actions, sort through difficult situations, and help you detect when course correction may be appropriate. An intentionality coach can be a friend, a therapist, a rabbi or priest or minister, a family member, or anyone who (1) makes you feel safe enough to be vulnerable with him or her, (2) understands and believes in what you are choosing to do, (3) has the courage to confront you when you are off-track, (4) will do it compassionately, and, most importantly, (5) is committed to living intentionally himself or herself.

- Do a midday check-in—When you stop for lunch, or midway through your day, check in with yourself. Rate yourself, on a scale of 1 (not at all) to 10 (consistently), on how well you have demonstrated your intentions through your actions.

STRATEGY #5. DO A COURSE CORRECTION.

Recognize you will frequently (and sometimes spectacularly) fail to live your life in alignment with your values and intentions. The issue is not how frequently you fall out of alignment, but whether or not you take the steps to re-calibrate your actions with your intentions. If you find you're off course:

- *Step one*: Determine if you can spot what took you off course—This isn't for purposes of assigning blame but rather to mark the danger spots for you the next time you pass that way. For some clients it is the nonverbal behaviors of others, such as a smirk or tears welling up in a loved one's eyes. For others, it is driven by internal needs such as wanting to impress an authority figure or avoid conflict. It can be physiological, such as low blood sugar from not having eaten, being exhausted, or having a tension headache that makes every interaction more difficult. Paying attention to when you do get off course allows you to be more prepared and thoughtful about when you take on potentially challenging conversations.

- *Step two*: Decide if there has been any collateral damage—If your "out of alignment" actions have impacted someone else, determine if an apology or other action is appropriate. A bank president I was working with faced a similar situation when, during our debrief of a conversation he had had with his direct reports, he realized he had been unintentionally abrasive. There is nothing like repeating the words you've used in a conversation to someone else to allow you to hear them for the first time! After our coaching session he immediately rounded his staff up and apologized to the group for his tone. He told me later they visibly relaxed in the meeting, thanking him repeatedly for his willingness to recognize a troubling behavioral pattern. My personal worst was the time I blew up at an ICU nurse for shaving Vito's mustache without telling me first. Although it seems unimportant now, at the time it represented to me, in a stark, visible manner, that my husband's illness from Guillain-Barré would be more long-term than I was ready to admit. It took me several hours to move past my self-righteous anger and realize I had not been the person I wanted to be in the exchange. My apology the next day changed the stiff professional dynamic we had both held onto for weeks into a warm, supportive one that nurtured both of us.

- *Step three*: Crystallize your new course in your mind—Decide what you would like to change about the event. What would you say differently? Do differently? Then, with as much detail as possible, imagine yourself going through the same event, this time handling it in the way you would like to. Repeat the same practice at least three times until the way you are imagining it feels possible, or perhaps manageable. This technique worked particularly well for a client of mine, Donna, who wanted to have a more adult relationship with her demanding and hypercritical sister. During our work together, the situation between Donna and her sister became exacerbated by her husband, Brad's, sudden, debilitating illness. Donna's sister had some extremely strong ideas about how Donna and Brad should handle his hospital stay and recovery and she was not in the least shy about sharing those ideas—undeterred by Donna's and Brad's desire to hear them. Donna's previous attempts to talk to her sister about being less intrusive had resulted in the sister becoming angry and hurt while Donna found herself shutting down and backtracking. Once Donna decided who she wanted to be with her sister in the upcoming conversa-tion—calm, nonjudgmental, candid, and firm—we wrote out a script:

Sis, I need to talk to you about something. Is now a good time? This recent crisis has been extremely hard on all of us and I want you to hear how much I appreciate the things you have done for us. [The sis-ter had cooked dinner for them, picked up prescrip-tions, and run household errands for them while they were at the hospital.] *I recognize how much you love Brad and me. As you are aware, there are a huge number of medical decisions to be made right now, with lots of information we have to sort through. Brad and I often feel overwhelmed by it. It would be most helpful to us right now if, when you have a different opinion of the course of treatment, you either keep it to yourself, or ask if we want to hear your thoughts. That way, we can let you know how open we are to hearing another opinion. This doesn't mean we don't value your thoughts. It just means when we are in overwhelm mode, one more opinion adds to a burden I believe you are trying to alleviate.*

We talked about how Donna would handle her sister's angry re-sponses or tears and how to continue to stay on her agenda rather than being dragged off topic by emotion or shutting down. Not sur-prisingly, her sister did blow up initially, feeling hurt and misunder-stood. Yet, as Donna continued to stay calm and appreciative of her sister but firm in her request, her sister grudgingly agreed to be less vocal about her opinions. Donna reported—for the first time in her life—she left a touchy conversation with her sister feeling older than four years old!

Step four: Move on. Do not waste time replaying the actual event in your head. This is not the performance you want to burn into your brain through repeatedly replaying it. For now, love the part of you who made the mistake because every part of you is lovable, not only the perfect parts. You are human. The mistake was about where you were, not who you are. Let it go, and move on with your life. Nothing more is to be gained by rehashing the event and your mis-steps.

CHAPTER 2:
CORRAL THE MIND MONKEYS

Life isn't as serious as the mind makes it out to be.
–Eckhart Tolle

I have entertained countless voices in my head—most of them nit-picking and critical. With everything to be done on a daily basis to assist Vito with his needs, pay loving attention to Nick, tend to clients, and stay connected to my lifelines of friends and family, the critical voices had enough material to write a musical. "You're not doing enough" was the choral refrain, but several other songs would emerge from time to time, usually highlighting some failure to be Superwoman in the lives of my family, clients, and friends.

Logically I knew I couldn't do it all. As I explored ways to handle those racing, generally critical thoughts crowding into my brain, I came across a Buddhist term for the mental chatter that immediately resonated—mind monkeys. Anyone who has ever been in a monkey house at the zoo understands the aptness of the term. Surrounded by monkeys of every size and kind, you are barraged by the unrelenting screams of the monkeys as they run up and down tree branches, swing from ropes, or climb the cages to examine the intruders into their domain. It is impossible to be heard over the ruckus and equally impossible to form any coherent thoughts, other than to flee.

Osho, an Eastern Buddhist philosopher, suggests taking a recorder, or a piece of paper, and capturing every single thought running through your head for the space of fifteen minutes and then analyz-ing it. It's surprising, once examined, to realize how repeatedly those thoughts are punitive, shaming, anxiety-provoking, and frequently demeaning. In fact, it is surprising how productive and sane most of us are, given the negative dialogue streaming through our heads.

Jon Kabat-Zinn, in *Full Catastrophe Living: Using the Wisdom of Your Body and Mind to Face Stress, Pain, and Illness*, talks about the variability of our thoughts and the emotions they engender. If you tried the experiment above, you may have noticed while some thoughts are neutral or positive, more frequently the thoughts are negative, bringing with them anxiety and fear. Kabat-Zinn points out that highly emotionally charged thoughts are more inclined to show up repeatedly and will "grab ahold of your attention like a powerful magnet, carrying your mind away from your breathing or from awareness of your body" (p. 343). When a crisis arrives in our lives, the negative thoughts can escalate and become debilitating. There are seemingly countless problems to solve and endless tasks and logistics to pay attention to; it feels impossible to control the stream of thoughts, much less turn it off. Yet this persistent inner dialogue keeps you from hearing your own wisdom, agitates your emotions, blows situations out of proportion, and can keep you from connecting with the love and support available to you. While completely controlling the thoughts can be highly difficult (if not impossible), we can become aware of the buzzing activity in our minds, recognize their impact on our stress levels, challenge and corral the thoughts, and gain some power over the persistent nature of the monkey mind.

STRATEGIES

STRATEGY #1. BECOME AWARE OF THE BABBLE IN YOUR HEAD.

The thoughts coursing through our heads are generally an unnoticeable backdrop to our days—so ingrained in our lives we accept them as truth, without challenging them. In order to become more intentional about what we let flood our psyches, we have to first become aware of the chatter. Try this method as a way of "tuning in" to your mind monkeys dialogue.

- *Step one*: Sit comfortably and set a timer for five minutes.

- *Step two*: Imagine you are an observer of your mind. Be curious, not judgmental, as you pay attention to the thoughts (or fragments of thoughts) and emotions flitting through your mind.

- *Step three*: Be curious about the nature of the thoughts. Are they logistical, critical, supportive, or anxious? Ultimately, are they helpful or distressing to you?

- *Step four*: When the timer goes off, write down on a piece of paper what you discovered.

STRATEGY #2. ANALYZE THE CHATTER.

A gifted coach and friend, Diane Marentette (coauthor of *A New Brain for Business: Leadership Practices That Unleash the Best from Your People and Your Business*), offers another version of sitting with the babble. Although it may be counterintuitive to the idea of corralling the mind monkeys, her experience was, whenever the mind noise seemed the loudest, there was usually something to learn. She would imagine catching one of the monkeys, bringing it face-to-face with her, and saying, "What? What are you trying to tell me?" She invariably found some important piece of information would come to mind, something hidden beneath the cacophony. The idea of mining the chatter for important information is similar to the recent phenomenon several of my clients who work in hedge funds have experienced. Because of the exploding amount of information available on the web, they're consistently overloaded with more data than they can reasonably sort through. One analyst in his late thirties shared with me he felt as if he spent his day "separating signal from noise"—meaning finding what was relevant out of the deluge of information coming his way. In these times of crisis, a good question to ask yourself is, what is relevant here? What will help me with this crisis or current situation? What is merely noise?

My clients have usually discovered, when the bulk of the thoughts whizzing around in their brains are negative, there is an unmet need hiding behind the noise. One client, whose wife was recovering from a serious, temporarily debilitating medical crisis, wrote down every single one of the anxious thoughts keeping him awake at night. As we examined the long list of household, financial, and medical concerns together, we were able to identify a critical issue for him he was ignoring—he did not feel he could ask his wife to handle any of the tasks, afraid any additional stress would set back her recovery. When we talked about it further, he began to realize his fears were based on where she had been several months previously but were no longer accurate. The whirling lists were actually his subconscious mind trying to get him to look at his feelings of being overwhelmed more logically.

STRATEGY #3. IDENTIFY AND RELEASE UNHELPFUL BELIEFS.

If you are like most people, you will find from the exercise above the majority of the thoughts in your head are critical, fearful, or anxious in nature. I view those fault-finding or fear-inducing thoughts as old lessons from my childhood, learned in hard and sometimes painful ways. Now, numerous years later, my younger self is trying its hardest to keep me out of trouble regardless of the fact the lessons are outdated. For example, the younger me who screams, "Be careful, they might get mad if you say that!" is not in on the fact I have had years of experience both delivering difficult messages and managing the fallout. It's true—the person I'm speaking to might get mad but the consequences of his or her anger are not what I experienced in childhood situations.

One of the first things I do when working with an anxious, fearful, or "stuck" client is to listen carefully to how she is describing her current situation. As I understand the outline of her dilemma, I begin to hear what was in her way in the past and is creating the issues now. The late Debbie Ford, in her book, *The Dark Side of the Light Chasers: Reclaiming Your Power, Creativity, Brilliance, and Dreams*, eloquently summed up the three major beliefs keeping people from successful, peaceful lives: "I might be abandoned," "I'm not good enough," and "I can't trust." It was her experience (and mine) that everyone carries one or more of these beliefs in their lives. The beliefs come from a variety of places: parental injunctions, siblings, school authorities, playground bullies, difficult experiences in childhood, and by observing others, to name a few. This is not to blame any of these people or experiences. Most of the beliefs we create in childhood are, in some way, useful for us at the time. The issue is when we continue to carry those beliefs into our adult years as they color, consciously and unconsciously, our interactions and decision-making—two areas of supreme importance when we are faced with a crisis.

One organizational client, Brad, was facing the terribly real potential of being fired from his Senior VP role in a retail company because of his caustic and know-it-all leadership style. He had alienated various peers by his putdowns and his need to appear an expert, even in areas where he knew little. We had worked together for a couple of weeks when I surprised him by suggesting his behavior seemed to be driven by a fear he wasn't actually "good enough" to be successful in his role. Brad vehemently denied was the issue, citing (again) his numerous accomplishments and credentials. Knowing he trusted his wife's perspective and pushing him further would be counterproductive to our early coaching relationship, I agreed I wasn't invariably right but asked him to find out what his wife, Jane, thought about my hypothesis. He readily agreed to do so, sure she would back his belief completely. Two weeks later when we met, I asked him about Jane's opinion. Sheepishly he admitted she had agreed with me and gone on to cite several examples in their married life where the same belief played out in unproductive ways.

Those core beliefs—"I'm not good enough," "I can't trust," and "I might be abandoned or rejected"—are customarily at the foundation of the monkey mind chatter, if you listen closely enough. Recognizing them for what they are, especially if they are old beliefs with no relevance to the current situation, allows you to make more intentional choices about your actions. Some important reflections:

- Where do your fearful, anxious, or critical thoughts come from? What old, worn-out stories might you be operating from? Are you the same person who adopted those beliefs originally or do you, too, have some new skills or perspectives, more relevant to who you are now?

- Ask yourself, "Do any of these stories sound like me?"

- Reflect back on a time recently where you were filled with anxiety about a decision or situation. Could the anxiety be tied to any of these stories?

- Ask a friend whom you trust if she or he sees one of these stories playing out in your life frequently.

Another way to handle the chatter is to capture a thought racing through your mind and ask yourself a simple question, "Is it true?" Is it true your friend will be horribly mad at you if you decide you're too tired to go to dinner? Are you sure? Chances are, if your friend truly cares about you, she knows you're under stress and, while she may be disappointed you can't join her for dinner, she will, in all likelihood, understand. There's a big difference between having a thought and assuming it is true. Or, as Byron Katie (*Loving What Is: Four Questions That Can Change Your Life*) puts it, "You either believe what you think or you question it. There's no other choice."

An example of challenging and releasing an old story was sent to me the other day by a client, a young man in his thirties who worked for a technology start-up company. Doug had been raised by a father who expected everyone to see life from the same perspective he did and any dissenting opinions were subjected to ridicule or icy silence. In our session, earlier in the week, we had discussed finding some healthy ways to de-stress and had decided to try watching a comedy as a way of relaxing with his family. Doug tried the experiment one evening and invited his family, including his father who was dining with them, to join him. Shortly after the movie started, his father left in a huff because he didn't approve of the film's storyline and salty language. It was then my client realized the extent to which his tastes in comedy (and several other areas of his life) had been dictated by his father's reactions. Once Doug challenged the unconscious thought that he could only like what his father liked, a new world of options opened up. He found it freeing to realize he could explore different kinds of comedies to determine what he liked, regardless of his father's opinion.

Recently, I've come to visualize old stories and beliefs as having an expired code date, like a bag of potato chips. While my clients may or may not be able to identify where the story came from, I encourage them to ask themselves, "Is this belief still accurate or has the code date expired?" Once a story or a belief is recognized as no longer true, I suggest they have a conversation with it: "Oh, hello, Mr. *I'm responsible for everyone's happiness in the room.* I'm afraid your code-date has expired. Goodbye!" Ask yourself:

- Which of your stories have expired code dates? What old stories or beliefs are no longer true?

- What can you say or do when you recognize an old, out-of-date story is influencing you? Clients have used a "drop kick" action to demonstrate their willingness to kick the old story to one side and try something new, or written down the out-of-date belief (once they realized it had shown up) and tossed it in the wastepaper basket, or told the story to "get out of here"—sometimes in more colorful language!

STRATEGY #4. RECRUIT A COMPASSIONATE VOICE.

A considerable number of my clients have grown up with harsh and critical parenting or other unsupportive early childhood experiences, and they struggle to comprehend how to speak kindly to themselves. One of the activities they find helpful is to imagine someone else who is completely supportive, giving them advice and counsel when they need it. In the early days of therapy, the voice they conjure up is usually mine, but I encourage them to find another personification of nurturing and care. Sometimes it's a guardian angel, a spirit guide, or a beloved parent, grandparent, or friend who has passed on. Oft times an image comes to them in meditation or prayer. One client, Linda, was married to an abusive, alcoholic husband. She came to therapy torn between leaving him to create a life congruent with her inner sense of joy and enthusiasm, and the fear of being on her own. As she sat still and turned inward, connecting to her heart, the image of her grandmother, a feisty straight-shooter came to her. We explored her relationship to her grandmother, wondering what kind of advice she would give, were she still alive. Laughing out loud for the first time since she arrived, she said, "Kick his butt out!" And even though it was several more months before she was ready to leave, Linda shared with me she periodically felt as if her grandmother was with her, giving her the courage to make the change. Finding the voice or essence of compassion is frequently the first step in my clients loving themselves.

- *Step one*: Close your eyes and reflect on who you've known, read about, or seen who exemplifies compassion or kindness to you.

- *Step two*: Pretend she or he is in the room with you, hearing the critical thoughts spoken out loud. What would your compassionate and supportive person do? Say?

- *Step three*: Write down some of the phrases you imagine your compassionate protector would say and keep them for the next time the mind monkeys start their fault-finding tirade.

A crisis brings hidden aspects of our lives to the surface—old stories and beliefs, fears and anxieties in particular. When we take the time to manage our thoughts, to stay present, and challenge the stories that are plaguing us, we begin to undergo a subtle change that can yield great benefits both during the crisis and afterwards.

CHAPTER 3:
WORK THROUGH THE FEAR

We must travel in the direction of our fears.
–John Berryman

Crises typically bring hard or terrifying experiences into our lives. We are stretched beyond our comfort zones time and again by the news we hear or the potential outcomes we face. Decisions have to be made when the choices are ugly or daunting and no one is available to take the blame away from us if we make the wrong choice. We can feel equally powerless when agreements are being made on a larger societal scale which could impact our lives in potentially disastrous ways—without our knowledge, input, or any viable recourse. During these times, we can find ourselves in situations that feel nightmarish—unexpected, full of frightening experiences, and fraught with anxiety. Those of us who have been frequent visitors to the land of nightmares have much to draw on during these times, if we will only remember.

Anyone who has ever had a nightmare has experienced the heart-stopping terror it brings. In nightmares we are pursued, put into danger, harmed, or faced with terrible choices. Although we are in a sleep state, our hearts pound, we shout out or flail around. Sometimes we feel frozen, unable to make a move to save ourselves or others. When we awaken, the dark around us still seems to hold the threat of further menace and our sense of safety is, at least for those first moments of consciousness, uncertain.

Having someone next to us who comforts us, listens to our fears, and dries our tears is wonderful, but not always possible. We also need a moment or two to regroup, make sense of the images still lingering, and sort out what is true from what were only the illusions of our mind. Leaving a nightlight on can help distinguish what is real from what is imagined more quickly. With reality more firmly in hand, people choose different paths. Some people, me included, lie quietly and reenter into the nightmare story in their minds. In those moments of quasi-sleep, I can save the children, stop the axe-wielding burglar, or find my classroom in time to take the final exam. Others choose to replace the images of terror with something more peaceful in order to truly let go of the nightmare and return to sleep.

The biggest problem with the barrage of ideas whirling ceaselessly in our minds is the anxiety and fear they can generate, particularly in crises. Fear disrupts your spiritual, emotional, and physical equilibrium and once it has done that, it keeps you from thinking straight. It is, as Harriet Lerner says in her book, *Fear and Other Uninvited Guests*, "a physiological process that cavorts and careens through our bodies and makes us miserable. Eventually, it subsides—only, of course, to return." Accepting that fear, terror, anxiety, and panic may happen in the course of a crisis can help you keep fear from taking control of your life. The strategies and ideas below are about navigating your way through fear when it arrives at your doorstep. Try them out and find the ones which work for you.

STRATEGIES

STRATEGY #1. STAY OUT OF DARK PLACES.

I believe staying calm and realistically optimistic allows us more mental capacity to maneuver. Spending an excessive amount of time with dark thoughts—which may or may not come true—creates a current reality for you which you certainly don't want to live in. Notwithstanding, if you will be in that spot one day, why go there any sooner than you have to? It's like realizing one day you will have to live somewhere you find totally abhorrent. It doesn't make sense, at least not to me, to vacation there repeatedly. Some ways to manage those thoughts include:

- Stay in the present moment—There are a variety of books out about staying in the present moment, Eckhart Tolle's *The Power of Now: A Guide to Spiritual Enlightenment* being one of the most recent and well-known. The concepts are simple—every time you find yourself ruminating on the future or the past, return your mind and your senses to the present. Executing the concepts takes practice and diligence. Nonetheless, any period of time you can keep your mind from traveling to the past or future is calming. Unless something bad or scary is happening to you at that precise moment, "now" is the safest place you can be.

- Leave the dark thoughts behind—One of my favorite things to do with children who are prone to nightmares is to have them write down their worries on a piece of paper before going to bed. Folding up the paper up and putting it away creates a visual to remind them they don't have to take their worry into their slumber. The same thing works for adults. Dumping the dark thoughts and scary scenarios out of our brains and onto paper, then literally burning the paper or putting the paper into a drawer, cabinet, or other space, can allow us to gain some breathing room.

- Focus on what you want instead—For some people, this idea may sound like encouraging someone to live in a fantasy world. We're taught we must face reality and deal with it rather than escaping from it. While I agree that dealing with unpleasantness when it occurs is part of our lives as responsible adults, as I've said earlier, I don't believe spending time worrying about what might happen makes any sense.

- Furthermore, making a practice of focusing on what you want, instead of what you don't want, as a way of working with the Divine to create your best possible good. Using visualization, pictures, affirmations, or journaling to imagine a peaceful or hopeful outcome, two things can happen. First, you begin to create a more positive mindset or at least provide yourself with a moment of distraction. Secondly, you let the Divine in on the future you choose to live in.

This practice is not a guarantee the outcome you are visualizing will happen, nor is it designed to be an invitation to ignore the facts or situations you must deal with in order to handle this crisis responsibly. Instead, it is intended to give you a break from the nightmarish "what ifs" and move you towards a potentially better place.

STRATEGY #2. FACE THE TERRIFYING QUESTIONS HEAD-ON.

If your thoughts are fear- or anxiety-driven but real possibilities, it can be significantly more difficult to manage their existence in your head. As much as I didn't want to look at the worst-case scenario with Nick's cancer diagnosis, the fact remained if eighty percent of the children with his disease were cured, twenty percent weren't. Fear had kept me from asking myself the one, crucial question—"could I be the mom Nick needed me to be, if the chemo didn't work?" The answer, when I finally summoned the courage to ask it of myself, was an unequivocal "yes."

The mind monkeys fell curiously silent as I acknowledged both my fear and my strength. Energy spent dodging the question was finally freed up, allowing me to focus on what had to be done. The possibilities were still there and were still terrifying, but I had built conviction in the one resource I had completely under control—myself. I could do this. If you find there is something draining your energy, try sitting still and answering the following:

- What's the most terrifying question you can ask yourself right now?

- What have you been avoiding looking at or facing?

- How much energy has it taken to suppress this question?

The importance of including others in the process of confronting the hard questions directly was brought home as I witnessed Dr. Michael Lerner, founder and leader of Commonweal Organization, lead a group of individuals living with cancer through a conversation about death. Several of the participants were in the final stages of their lives while others were in recovery from the disease. Yet everyone one of them commented about the relief and sense of healing they felt—talking about death. It was a conversation few of them had been able to have with their loved ones, leaving the elephant in the room, stinky and unacknowledged. While you may not be dealing with end-of-life issues, consider these questions as well, as you explore the hard and scary places in your life:

- Are there conversations you could be having which you are afraid to have?

- What is the cost of avoiding the conversation? To you or your loved ones?

- What would be the first step you could take towards initiating the discussion?

- Is there someone who can help you have it or at least practice it?

- If the other person is unwilling to talk, is there another way to work through this issue? If you need some assistance, find a trusted professional with whom you can examine the issues you feel are important to be discussed. Therapists, ministers, rabbis, and social workers are typically trained specifically to help people have difficult conversations. Furthermore, they can facilitate those conversations with you and the people whom you love.

STRATEGY #3. SCHEDULE YOUR FEAR.

Early in my therapy career I was honored to work with some survivors of torture. One client was a wonderful and inspiring twenty-five-year-old woman who had been captured by guerrilla fighters at eighteen. At their hands, Ayshah had been raped, tortured, and lost her unborn child. A devout Muslim, she had made peace with her experience and forgiven her captors, knowing bitterness would ruin the life she had been able to make away from her homeland. Ayshah came to therapy with persistent, troubling thoughts—not about her torture, as I had anticipated, but about her fears for her family, still living in the African country where she had been born. She was rarely able to make contact with her family and found her entire day was repeatedly taken up by petrifying thoughts, distracting her from the joy and responsibilities of her newborn child.

As a faithful follower of her religion Ayshah prayed five to seven times a day and so we devised a schedule for her fears, tying it to her spiritual life. She set the timer for ten minutes prior to the prayer time. During those ten minutes, Ayshah concentrated solely on her thoughts and worries about her family, wondering how they were doing, allowing her imagination to have full control of where her thoughts went. Then, when the timer went off, indicating the end of the "worry time," Ayshah would unroll her prayer rug, say her prayers, and hand her family over to the loving embrace of Allah. Within a short time Ayshah reported her worry had diminished significantly, flaring up only when international news was particularly dire or rumors from her community triggered the anxious thoughts.

My clients typically find it works best to schedule the time for anxious thoughts during a regularly occurring event—such as while exercising or driving to and from work. Once the time is set there is a process that seems to work, but it does take practice.

When the anxious thoughts come up, catch yourself and say (out loud, if possible), "Stop!" Remind yourself you are going to stew over this topic or situation only during the scheduled time. I suggest to my clients they talk to the thought as if they were talking to a child. "I'm sorry, *what will I do if I lose my job* (or whatever fear you are facing), you are not scheduled for another four hours. Please feel free to return at six p.m. when I am driving home from work."

- Each time the thought returns, repeat the conversation. It will take a while to catch yourself (and you'll be surprised by how sneaky the thought is) but if you continue to stop the thought and reschedule it, the recurrence of the anxious thoughts will go down significantly.

- At the scheduled time, be sure to allow the thoughts to arise, and ruminate on the issue, if you so desire. Remember, though, to wind it down once your scheduled time is over.

The idea of thought-stopping is not a new one—it is integral to a form of psychotherapy called Cognitive Behavioral Therapy. CBT focuses on the relationship between your thoughts and how you feel or behave. Yet there are times during a crisis when situations that can engender anxiety must be considered. The issue comes when we spend more time on those thoughts than is either healthy or needed. Scheduling the thoughts allows you to limit the amount of time spent in fear or anxiety. And, you may find, as my clients do, once you've learned how to stop and redirect the thoughts, your desire to fret about the situation diminishes significantly—during and outside of those scheduled times.

STRATEGY #4. MOVE FROM PARALYSIS INTO AC-TION.

As mentioned previously, by writing our fears down and speaking them out loud, we begin to settle our brains for the problem-solving process. Use this process to help your amygdala calm down and engage the analytical part of your brain.

- *Step one*: Go someplace quiet and make a list, in detail, of your worst fears about the crisis you are facing. Put them in column form with space for another column next to each item.

- *Step two*: Read them out loud, slowly, letting them sink in. Then, read them again and again until the emotional punch behind the fear starts to diminish. Breathe deeply and slowly to allow the emotions to be released from your body.

- *Step three*: In the column next to your fear, write down three practical tactics or action items you would need to take if your fear were to come true.

Save the information and the next time the fearful thought arises, reread it or remind yourself you have an action plan.

If I am working with a client who is fearful the downsizing her company is going through will include her, we would start by writing her fear down. Next we explore if there are any other fears associated with the initial fear. Commonly, this includes financial fears as well as the implications for her family—feeling like a failure, or not being able to afford after-school activities. Once the fears are written down, we go through each fear and talk about what she could do, if the job loss were to come to pass. For example, if the biggest fear is actually finances (and frequently the first fear named is not the most critical), we outline steps she might take now as well as if she is laid off. Being proactive by finding out if she has a clause in her home-owner's policy covering mortgage payments in case of layoffs, cutting down on her spending and/or paying off credit cards, and talking to a financial advisor are ways she could take some steps which will put her in a better place, should she be laid off. Secondly, we would outline the most critical steps (with regard to her financial fears) she could take if she loses her job. It would depend on the situation but it might include downsizing her home and exploring ways to significantly cut her spending by working with a financial counselor. The answers are different for everyone. The trick is, by taking action, you can move out of "freeze" mode and into productive behavior.

STRATEGY #5. BE GRATEFUL.

It's hard to believe a serious life crisis and the word "blessing" would come in the same sentence. To some, the idea of looking for something positive in Nick's and Vito's cancer diagnoses might have seemed hyper-religious or Pollyannaish in the extreme. Spiritually, I viewed it as a form of radical surrender to an organizing framework of my life; practically, it kept me sane.

Research bears out the importance of gratitude. The Greater Good Science Center, citing the research of more than thirty scientists and graduate students, has found gratitude impacts not only our emotions with increased happiness, joy, optimism, compassion, and generosity, it can also lower blood pressure and improve the immune system. Robert Emmons, a leading expert on gratitude, suggests using a visual cue (such as a picture or a sticky note) to remember to take the time to be grateful, keeping a gratitude journal, or learning prayers of thankfulness as ways to incorporate more gratitude into your life. Regardless of how you choose to incorporate it into your daily living, find a time every day to look for opportunities to be grateful. I used the travel time from work to home to name the things I was grateful for each day. It not only made my commute better but allowed me to arrive at home in a substantially better mood.

- Ask yourself, "What are you grateful for? What kindnesses have others done for you? What went well (or at least better than you thought)? If nothing comes to mind, take a moment to be grateful for the simple things—food in your stomach, a soft place to lay your head, eight uninterrupted hours of sleep.

- Rick Hanson (*Buddha's Brain: The Practical Neuroscience of Happiness, Love, and Wisdom*) suggests "taking in the good" as a way to counter the brain's natural tendency to hang on to the negative thoughts and to quickly let go of the positive ones. Whenever something good happens, he suggests you first fully experience it. Notice the sky is bright blue after a week of clouds or the delightful smell of fresh-baked cookies in the bakery you've just passed. Focus your mind fully on the experience. Second, keep your attention on the positive experience. If your mind tries to shift away, bring it back to the deliciousness of what you are thinking, feeling, sensing, seeing, or touching. Finally, visualize those lovely thoughts, sensations and emotions flowing into your entire body. Imagine them and feel them filling you up until you are full to the brim with what this experience has to offer.

The process of regaining your balance after you've been plunged into a crisis is one where intention meets discipline. Intention allows us to take control of those aspects we can personally impact. When we focus inward on who we want to be, instead of blaming or looking to others to fix our problems, we find new degrees of freedom to replace those which may be temporarily unavailable to us. For those of us who have unusually active minds, prone to overthink or obsess when we are facing new or difficult challenges, discipline is the secret weapon. With focused attention and effort, our thoughts can serve us well. Problem solving, working through logistics, researching and understanding data, and assimilating new information are only a few ways our minds can assist us when we are going through a crisis. This is an important place to be intentional in your approach. Without the discipline of corralling our thoughts and facing our fears, though, the mind can become the crisis's henchman—there to make our challenges more dire, the options hellish, and the outcomes pessimistic. Please return to this chapter whenever the chatter of the mind monkeys and the force of fear threatens to overwhelm you. The information to help you get back on track is here.

THE THIRD STAGE: GATHER YOUR RESOURCES

*Let today be the day you learn the grace of letting go and
the power of moving on.*
–Steve Maraboli

By the time you've made it to this stage, you presumably have gone through the initial shakeup this event brought into your life. You've hopefully found a sense of balance, no matter how small, in setting your intentions and dealing with the problems this crisis has brought. It's time to move forward into the day-to-day struggles and challenges a crisis brings.

In my years working with clients I have found a few people who appear to effortlessly do this. They take stock of what needs to be done, what assistance or resources they may need, and set off in the direction which makes the most sense to them. Usually, the process of moving forward comes more slowly. Clients spend time longing for the pre-crisis days, hanging on to the hope that, somehow, a time machine will take them back to B.C.—Before Crisis. This makes sense to me. Crises can bring huge losses and challenges into our daily existence and there is comfort remembering easier times.

But looking backwards can make it difficult to move forward, much less plan the best path. I met a woman who, five years after her husband's death, still had his clothes in their master bedroom closet. She had decided she would create a quilt from those clothes for their infant son's bed—a way to surround him with what was physically left of his father. And despite the fact it sounded like a heartfelt project, I wondered if the planned quilt was, in reality, an elegant form of denial and her procrastination an effective method of keeping herself from moving forward.

Yet setting out precipitously, without preparing thoughtfully for the journey ahead, can result in disaster. Crises can bring long-term reverberations into our lives and knowing the resources we can rely on allows us to make decisions more intentionally. I have found two of the most important criteria for moving forward effectively are acceptance of the current reality and recognition of the resources you have available for you on the journey.

For me, one of the most effective ways I had to handle the seemingly constant shifts, challenges, and losses Vito's and Nick's medical diagnoses dropped into our lives was to accept, for right then, these crises *were* our family's "real" lives and we were ultimately the ones who would be living it. Time spent wishing things were different only brought more discomfort. I kept going back to Byron Katie's words, in her book *Four Questions That Can Change Your Life*, "I am a lover of what is, not because I'm a spiritual person, but because it hurts when I argue with reality." With reality acknowledged, I could turn my energy and attention to what I needed to get Vito, Nick, and myself through the days ahead.

CHAPTER 1:
LEVERAGE YOUR STRENGTHS

Finding the center of strength within ourselves is in the long run the best contribution we can make to our fellow men.
–Rollo May, *Man's Search for Himself*

A few years ago, I began the process of interviewing senior business leaders who had experienced cancer. Generously, leaders from business, government, non-profits, and the judiciary met with me to talk about their dances with cancer and the wisdom they had learned on their journey. As I began to look back over my notes, one of the themes which emerged was the deftness with which they made use of their natural strengths as leaders. The capabilities they brought to their cancer fight were, in a large part, the competencies which had made them successful leaders—focus, discipline, delegation, communication, and other important leadership skills. It was if, in the moments following their diagnosis, they instinctively knew the assets within them they could rely on in this crisis.

What are strengths? Marcus Buckingham, in *Go Put your Strengths to Work*, suggests strengths have three components: talents you are born with, skills you have learned, and knowledge acquired through education, training, or experience. In order to leverage your strengths in a crisis, you first have to figure out what they are. Once identified, you can begin to recognize how those strengths might help you in this current crisis.

STRATEGIES

STRATEGY #1. CHECK YOUR LIFE-SKILLS PANTRY.

Our strengths don't disappear in a crisis. The talent, skills, and abilities which have helped you be successful in your life up until now can be a platform to help you stay sane and functional during a crisis. As you take stock of your strengths, reflect back on the times in which you've had to get through a difficult task in your life. Some questions to ask yourself:

- During the earlier crisis or challenge, how did you cope? What did you do? Who helped you through the challenge? What worked and what didn't? Although this crisis may be a more intense or scary situation than those, some of the same actions can work.

- Get someone who knows you well to analyze your strengths with you. Determine how those strengths can be used in this crisis to accomplish what needs to be done and maintain your own energy and spirit. Recruit family and friends to help you think this through, if possible.

- Take a StrengthsFinder, or similar, online test. (www.strengthsfinder.com) It is Buckingham's contention you can identify a strength by recognizing those things you 1) do successfully, 2) do instinctively, 3) enjoy doing, and 4) feel fulfilled by having done it. Using this, or a similar personality inventory, can be one way to identify yours. Decide if what emerges can be utilized now.

Write the strengths down and say them out loud. Share your strengths with others, or make it into an affirmation or mantra. With the demands you are facing, it's easy to forget you are a person with skills and abilities. One of my coaching clients was brilliant at attacking an issue with every ounce of his intelligence, skills, and personal will. When he was going through cancer, his mantra was "hit it hard." How will you hold onto your strengths in the days ahead?

STRATEGY #2. KNOW YOUR BLIND SPOTS.

No one is good at everything but where we can create big problems in our lives are our blind spots. Most of us have had the experience of starting to move into the traffic lane next to us and abruptly being aware of another car in that lane. There will be skills and abilities you will need you currently don't have. Knowing what they are gives you a chance to plan around them by recruiting or paying for help from others who possess the skills you don't. The blind spots in our lives are usually psychological—such as being unwilling to admit we don't have the expertise or skill set to handle a particular issue. They can also be a fear or a prejudice that causes us to react inappropriately in certain situations. Consistently, I find my clients' blind spots can be instrumental in creating the crises in their lives or making a problem larger than it actually is. The crisis you are dealing with is already demanding; identifying your potential blind spots can be a strategy to help you minimize the challenges. And, as with driving, in order to reduce the possibility of collisions, it is helpful to have the mirrors positioned correctly, look over our shoulders, and, when possible, detect where danger might be imminent.

- Look at past situations where you were surprised by an outcome—something you didn't see coming but had a significant repercussion. In hindsight, what did you miss? How might similar surprises play out in this current situation and what can you do to avoid it or reduce the likelihood of it happening again?

- Enlist friends who know you well and who have navigated through crises of their own. Ask them to brainstorm ideas with you. It can be hard to have someone tell you about your blind spots so pick friends who have your best interests in mind and will handle this process compassionately.

STRATEGY #3. WATCH FOR OVERUSED STRENGTHS.

One of the most common reasons I am asked to coach senior executives is overused strengths. The competitiveness that made them the top salesperson in their firm can create dissent among direct reports who feel as if they have a competitor for a boss rather than someone who is developing or guiding them. Similarly, I found I had to dial down my energetic (perhaps somewhat obsessive) monitoring of Vito's recovery once he again became competent to handle his medical team.

You may find your strengths can be overused or perhaps become an obstacle under certain circumstances during this crisis. Kaiser and Kaplan, in a 2009 Harvard Business Review article,[13] addressed this topic as it pertained to leaders. Their finding was "the more pronounced your natural talent and the stronger your strengths, the graver the risk of taking them to counterproductive extremes." For example, my client who used his focus and determination to "hit it hard" during his cancer also shut out family and friends who wanted to support him during his treatment. He admitted, if he were to be diagnosed with cancer again, he would want to balance his approach more, and let others be there for him. Be aware of your default tendencies (the strengths you immediately utilize when faced with a challenge) and stay tuned into feedback from others or the environment itself which might indicate it's time to try a different approach or new strategies.

You, like everyone, have natural skills, talents, and knowledge—strengths and wisdom that will serve you during this crisis. After you've regained your balance, remembering and leveraging your strengths intentionally can be a starting place for moving forward. Staying in tune with your wisdom and the natural shifts occurring as part of the challenge you are going through allow your strengths to remain an asset rather than become a liability. Starting with what you naturally bring to a crisis and supplementing it by thoughtfully bringing others in allows you to magnify your strengths and fill in the gaps between where you are and where you are going.

CHAPTER 2:
CREATE A COMMUNITY
OF SUPPORT

*A friend is someone who knows the song in your heart
and can sing it back to you when you have forgotten the
words.*
–Unknown

Community, necessary to our survival in normal situations, becomes essential during times of crisis. Most simply, in a crisis we need 1) help getting things done, 2) particular kinds of knowledge or expertise we do not have but which are crucial to resolving the crisis, and 3) emotional, spiritual, or physical support. Getting things done can include everything from assistance clearing out debris when a tornado has destroyed your yard, transportation to doctors' appointments, help filling out insurance forms, mowing a lawn, or contacting the right people to get an issue resolved.

In a crisis, we may need access to expertise and information not already part of our personal skill set. We need lawyers to advise us on wills or other legal procedures, medical specialists to explain medical options and potential outcomes, psychologists to assess and advise on appropriate treatments for mental conditions, and consultants to bring specialized information forward to help us answer questions or choose between difficult options. We need people in our lives who will remind us of who we are and of what we are truly capable; who will hold us and our hope when it has slipped our grasp. And, like any precious resource, we are best served when we put as much attention into sustaining our community of support as we do into creating it.

STRATEGIES

STRATEGY #1. SELECT YOUR COMMUNITY THOUGHTFULLY.

Approach the idea of building a community of support as if you were the CEO of a small startup company assembling a board of directors to advise it. What will this "company" need to make it through the initial crisis stage of a startup and become a healthy and thriving organization?

This happens frequently when a loved one dies. Someone in the family typically steps up to organize logistics—from contacting the funeral home through the day of the funeral and beyond. Family and friends are assigned tasks based on their availability, expertise, or skills. Having a community of support in place brings both emotional comfort and tactical organization at a time when the bereaved are usually functioning on autopilot.

- *Step one*: When the crisis hits tsunami levels, take a few moments to consider what support you need. Make a to-do list of what has to be done, without finalizing about the "who" part of the equation. Some questions to ask yourself:

  o What is on there you dread taking on? Where do you feel clueless?

  o What are the problems requiring solutions or the decisions needing to be made? What kinds of expertise or knowledge will be critical in understanding the options – costs, benefits, and potential consequences?

- ○ Is it expertise you don't have, information you can't get access to, a listening ear, someone to remind you of who you are beneath the emotions and details you have to handle?

- *Step two*: Now determine who can provide what you need. Don't try to find one person to take care of every one of your needs; rather, make a list of people who have a portion of those qualities. If it is expertise you and your normal circle of support don't possess, then begin to brainstorm (preferably with a friend and trusted adviser):

  - ○ How can you research the potential universe of experts? Where is that information available? Who among your group of friends or acquaintances might have the knowledge you require?

  - ○ What are your criteria for a consultant, lawyer, doctor, or specialist? What is a "must have" versus a "nice to have"?

Perhaps because of my age or the age of a large percentage of my clients, one of the most common places where I observe people engaging support outside of their usual circle of family and friends is when moving an aged parent into assisted living. All at once, there are questions to be answered and action steps to be taken completely out of their area of competence, even for the highly skilled and competent professionals I see in my practice. By seeking out those who specialize (either professionally or through personal experience) in organizing, moving, finding appropriate facilities, and engaging physicians with geriatric specializations, their anxiety lessens, allowing them to focus on their loved ones more completely.

STRATEGY #2. SHAPE THE SUPPORT YOU WANT.

One of the most valuable things you can do when pulling together a support team is to let them clearly understand how they can help you best. When people are providing assistance to someone, they want to feel they are doing it "right" – which requires knowing what "helpful" looks like to you. You know yourself best and can provide them with clarity about what you need. Don't make them guess and take the chance of getting it wrong. While the particulars will presumably vary depending on the issue for which you are seeking help, the individual providing it, and where you are—physically, emotionally, psychologically, evaluate:

- Format—what form of communication works best for you? Email, text? Phone calls? Face to face? Facebook messaging?

- Timing—When are you most available? How quickly do you need the assistance?

- Detail—Do you need all the facts, where the information comes from, backup data? Or only the bottom line?

One of my closest friends told me, years after I first shared Nick's diagnosis, how much she appreciated my note telling her to email me, instead of call. (I remember my exact words were, "Send me emails, please, Barbara. If I hear your voice, I'm sure I'll cry.") I knew while I was doing everything I could to keep it together for Nick, I couldn't handle actually hearing Barbara's nurturing, loving voice without completely breaking down.

STRATEGY #3. PRESERVE YOUR COMMUNITY.

As important as it is to gather, shape, and effectively leverage your community of support, it is equally important to maintain it. It's easy, when you're the one suffering, to turn your support system into a dumping place for your angst and anger. It would be normal for this to happen on occasion but, when balanced with staying connected, demonstrating appreciation, and providing some kind of reciprocity (when possible), the support system is more apt to stay in place without burning out or experiencing compassion fatigue. Some ways to preserve your community include:

- Keep them informed. When people have invested in helping you through a crisis, it is only natural to want to be up-to-date on what is happening in your life. Make sure they are kept up-to-date. They will appreciate knowing but will also be in a better place to help you if their information is current. I was later told the structure I used in the emails I sent was helpful. Starting the emails with the facts, I followed with my thoughts, beliefs, and where we were emotionally. My finishing words told them we would be okay—we had the resources to make it through. My friends told me the emails' structure allowed them to take a small portion of our journey with us, touching both their heads and hearts.

- Say thank you. Consider ways to show appreciation and gratitude for what they are doing and have done. It can be as easy as keeping stationery or an electronic tablet with you so whenever time allows you can jot a quick note expressing your heartfelt gratitude for their assistance and help. One client threw a party for his support system once the crisis had abated, as a way to publicly recognize the time and energy so freely given to him.

- Be interested in their lives. Stay genuinely connected; ask about their families. Make sure they feel comfortable about their own lives by giving them permission (encouraging them, in fact) to talk about what is going on for them. Frequently people would apologize to me for whining about their child's poor grades or a problem at the job. My answer was I wanted to hear, sometimes needed to hear, about their lives. They were important to me. Take the time to ask and listen.

Early into the crisis, you might also want to say to those important to you something like "I'm pretty sure, while I go through this, at some point I'm going to be grumpy, moody, distant, or sarcastic. I want to apologize to you in advance. Please point it out when I do it because it's not who I want to be, but also please understand it is not personal." Or when your friends tell you they fear you will "lose it" during the crisis, you might want to respond with, "I hope not, but if I do, please forgive me. It won't be about you."

STRATEGY #4. KEEP SIGHT OF YOUR WISDOM.

As comforting as it may feel, when you are working with an expert, to hand over a decision or let someone else determine the path you will take during this crisis, you are ultimately responsible for what happens. When you have been given advice, take time to sit with the information or advice you are given. Check in with your body for its wisdom—does what they are saying "feel" right? I find I feel relaxed and light when a decision makes sense to me but the area around my heart, through to my back, tenses up and feels uncomfortable when I'm hearing something that doesn't resonate for me. Paying attention to your own signals can provide a quick, useful way to gauge how you genuinely feel about what you are being told. If you can't get a clear read, ask for more time to sit with the information. When I was asked for permission to put in a gastric feeding tube into Vito, my initial gut reaction was an immediate (and fear-based) "no!" Luckily for me, Vito's extraordinarily kind pulmonologist suggested I consider it overnight before making the final decision. Away from the tubes, monitors, and overwhelming urgency of the ICU, I sat with the idea. As my fear receded, I checked in with my own deep wisdom, and found the courage to say "yes."

Keep in mind, when hiring a professional, it is our job to decide if they meet our needs. It's important to ask ourselves if they are the right fit for not only this crisis but for us. As you talk to them about working with you through this crisis, explain what the relationship would look like to you, listen deeply to their responses to your questions and your preferences, and, if possible, take some time deciding if they and what they tell you resonates with your sense of what is needed.

Another way to stay connected to your wisdom is by enlisting a friend to help you do so. I, like a large number of therapists, believe in the power of compelling questions. When used appropriately, they open up space for the individual's intuition and inner wisdom to emerge. Inviting a trusted friend to pose questions to help you deliberate on an issue is quite different than asking them what you should do. In fact, if you choose to do this, it may be helpful to do this in two parts. First, they will ask questions to help you clarify your own reasoning and secondly, they can offer you any thoughts that come to them after you have finished the clarification process. Here's how to proceed:

- *Step one*: Clarify your reasoning—have your friend present the questions in Appendix B (or a subset of them) for forty-five minutes while you respond out loud or make notes about what comes to you. If your response generates a follow-up question from your friend, request they suspend their thoughts until the end.

- *Step two*: Offering their thoughts—This is where your friend can share what has come to him or her as s/he has heard you explore the situation. Remember, you are not asking them for advice, rather to offer what comes to them. When you ask someone what to do, they may pull back out, fearful of steering you incorrectly, especially when a huge decision must be made. Some ways to elicit thoughts include:

  o   What do you hypothesize I may be missing?

  o   What else would you want to learn before making this decision?

  o   What do you hear from me that concerns you?

It is truly a gift to have a well-crafted community of friends, experts, and supporters who stand next to you while you are navigating your way through the innumerable challenges, upsets, and decisions a crisis brings. In some ways, it's similar to the days of pioneers—a community coming together to raise a barn, celebrate a harvest, or mourn a friend. We are part of a whole and it is in crisis we can feel the absence or presence of those other parts of the whole most keenly. But the reach of our community has expanded exponentially from the pioneer days, especially with the Internet. In times of crisis, it is especially important to navigate that resource intentionally.

CHAPTER 3:
USE THE INTERNET...CONSCIOUSLY

The Internet is becoming the town square of the
global village of tomorrow.
–Bill Gates

The variety and number of social media tools currently available is staggering to those of us born in the fifties and sixties. Facebook, near the end of 2016, had close to 2 billion users who were active on a monthly basis. In addition to social networking sites such as Facebook, a quick Google search found ten different categories of social media sites ranging from publishing tools (such as blogs) to photo-sharing sites (such as Instagram) to virtual worlds (such as Farmland). For a growing number people, the community where they are most active is Internet-based. Yet, while the social media can be a critical component in finding the assistance, resources, and support you need during a crisis, it also has the potential to be used in ways which are ultimately detrimental.

This dichotomy has never been, at least to me, as obvious as during the 2016 elections. Between the pervasive "reporting" of fake news, social media postings of snippets of real stories being blown out of proportion or taken out of context, and Facebook friends sniping or complaining about candidates, it was difficult to ascertain what was true, much less helpful about social media in determining which candidate to choose. Post-election, websites, Twitter, and Facebook pages (among others) have provided a safe place for some to vent but may have escalated a sense of outrage or despair for others.

So how do you harness the possibilities inherent in this global village without creating more suffering for yourself or others? The answer, again, is about taking thoughtful, conscious actions aligned with your intentions. Having and following a strategy, as well as monitoring the reactions you have to your time on social media, allows you a measure of control that may prevent future disappointments or anxiety.

STRATEGIES

STRATEGY #1. HAVE A SOCIAL MEDIA PLAN

Discernment is important with regard to both the content and the amount of content you choose to take in. During a crisis, you will undoubtedly to be called upon to make various important decisions. Allowing yourself to be overloaded by unimportant information or the kind of trivia frequently found on social networking sites can use up a valuable resource—your attention. Joseph M. Kayany, Ph.D., in his paper "Information Overload and Information Myths,"[14] suggests whichever way you define information overload, the ability to make a solid, effective decision comes down to four components: the quality of the information, the amount of information, the time available to process and synthesize the information, and an individual's cognitive capacity. In a crisis, the last two (time available and cognitive capacity) could easily be impacted adversely, making how much information you seek out, as well as the actual quality of the information (getting facts from well-vetted sites and rather than from a personal blog, for example) all the more important.

When using social media as a method to build a community of support during this time, decide first what type of support you hope the social media tool will provide. It is important to remember you may be at your most vulnerable during a crisis, and, at least at the beginning of the crisis, possibly making decisions based more on short-term reactions and emotions than a long-term analysis of what you need. One way to begin to find your way through these questions of what you need from social media is to conceptualize it as a way to both "take in" content as well as "reach out" to others.

STRATEGY #2 REGULATE WHAT YOU TAKE IN.

When you are taking in content—for example, through others' blogs, following people on Twitter, looking at Facebook posts, reading informational websites, or watching educational or inspirational YouTube videos—consider both the facts you are looking for as well as the way in which it could impact your mood. Ask yourself:

- Which sources will give me helpful information as I navigate through this crisis?

- Are there experts, thought leaders, or spiritual advisers who can inspire or encourage me?

- Will this information help me make better decisions or handle the crisis in a more positive manner (if this is your goal)?

- How do I feel after I've "taken in" this content? More capable or more anxious? Uplifted or more vulnerable?

STRATEGY #3. DECIDE WHO TO INVITE IN.

It is becoming more and more prevalent for people going through crises to use social media as a way to "reach out"—which can have both positive and negative consequences. Writing a blog, or updating your status on CaringBridge or on other social media tools, can keep your friends and family informed as well as provide the release and clarity expressive writing can bring. So, what could be wrong with posting your difficulties with your marriage, your fears about having enough money to retire, or asking for help in looking for a job? First, depending on the site, you may be assuming everyone who reads your post or blog is willing to meet you where you are during this crisis. For example, millions of people turn to Facebook for amusement, distraction, to further a personally important agenda, or to catch up on the lives of their friends. If they have no personal investment in you, they may not respond in a supportive or helpful way to you. So, how should you reach out into a community for support? Sit with your emotions for a while before reaching out. In the moments of stillness, ask yourself what you need from this virtual community.

- People who completely "get" what you are going through? Finding online support groups composed of people who are going through the same kind of crisis as you may be the best place for you to land. For example, Google "newly divorced dad" and "online support" and hundreds of thousands of results (or more) will come up—including forums, blogs, and a multitude of other resources.

- A way to inform people so they can avoid the same crisis or get through it more effectively? If so, consider carefully 1) the best forum (social networking, blogging, etc.) and 2) giving people the opportunity to "opt in" or "opt out" of the content you are offering. For example, providing a link to your blog or resources that have helped you allows readers to decide how much information they want on the subject versus assuming if it was helpful to you it will be equally important to them (How many of us have "unfriended" or hidden posts from friends whose never-ending political diatribes have grown old? I have, particularly during major election years).

- People who will support you unconditionally during this crisis? Despite its appearance, Facebook is not an intimate community of caring people. It is a place where people typically share the fairly trivial, commonplace, or daily thoughts, activities, and events of their lives. In the emotion-laden climate of a crisis, a sense of vulnerability can arise, creating for some a heightened need for external validation or understanding. Unless your online community is composed solely of individuals who love and support you already, you may be looking for "likes" in all the wrong places.

- A place to vent or be validated? Consider whether or not social media is the safest place for venting to occur. And, are you emotionally in the right place to do so? Are you going to post something future employers might read? Will your kids' friends see it or have access to it? Are you saying something to put another person in a negative light (and could perhaps make you liable for slander should s/he find out?) How will you feel if someone responds negatively to this baring of your soul? And, do you want someone else's validation to have more power than your own internal wisdom?

A friend who is a compelling and inspirational speaker shared with me her amazement at watching numerous of her fellow speakers at a large national conference with over 20,000 attendees step off a podium and immediately check Facebook to find out what the attendees had said about their speeches. She had done the same, despite receiving a rousing, standing ovation for a speech she knew had been the best in her life. She recognized, in her moment of human need for validation, she had unconsciously discounted her inner knowing and subtly undermined her belief in herself.

Interestingly, the research on the impact of Facebook and other social networking sites has demonstrated both positive as well as negative impacts on users.[15] While some studies have found positive status updates appear to encourage others to post similarly positive updates, other researchers have found data to suggest spending time on Facebook leads users to compare their lives unfavorably to their friends, making them feel less upbeat or confident in themselves.[16] Consequently, while social media can be both an effective way to meet certain support needs and give you a sense of community, as well as provide an attractive distraction from the day-to-day struggles challenges can bring, using it thoughtfully is the key.

You bring all of yourself into each phase of your dance with the crisis you are experiencing. We are an amalgam of our experiences, our beliefs, our expertise, our weaknesses, and our strengths. Bringing those consciously forward, and inviting, wooing, or paying others to supplement what you have with what you need, allows you to accomplish the Herculean tasks ahead. I was reminded of this by a note, left at Vito's bedside by a friend to remind Vito (and us) of our strengths, which made me cry. The quote comes from A.A. Milne's magical book, *Winnie the Pooh,* and is a quote from Christopher Robin to Pooh. I hope you will find in it the solace and inspiration we did.

If ever there is tomorrow when we're not together…there is something you must always remember. You are braver than you believe, stronger than you seem, and smarter than you think. But the most important thing is, even if we're apart…I'll always be with you.

THE FOURTH STAGE: CRAFT A NEW NORMAL

The secret of change is to focus all of your energy, not on fighting the old, but on building the new.
–Socrates

Anyone who has ever been a parent of an infant understands the concept of making a "new normal" work. In the first few months of life, one single goal becomes primary in the lives of a freshly minted parent—nurturing a brand-new life. Unfamiliar roles and competencies are required, relationships are strained, and sleep is no longer a given. Clear communication, multitasking, and a sense of humor go far in the new existence children bring to our lives. There can be losses to be dealt with as well: friends who can't make the shift to a family-friendly life, the freedom childlessness allows, time and closeness with significant others, and our own senses of identity—who we were "before."

Crises are not as joyful as the arrival of a child, but they can definitely be as disruptive. Being intentional about what is important, what needs to be released, focusing on what works, and nurturing yourself in the process make the path to the new normal smoother.

In order to create a life designed to sustain you as you continue through this middle period of your crisis, you must make space for that life. Release the things no longer working in the present situation and find ways to tend to your needs as the crisis continues. The process of releasing takes time—time to recognize what you've been holding onto, to evaluate its fit in your present life, and the space to mourn for what you must let go of, if only temporarily. You also must find ways to keep yourself whole, conscious, and intentional, maintaining your reserves to meet the needs before you.

CHAPTER 1:
UNPACK YOUR BAGS

People do not always make breakthroughs because they refused to quit. Sometimes they make them because they know when to quit. When they realize that enough is enough, that old patterns aren't serving them, that it's time to repack their bags.
–Richard J. Leider

Richard J. Leider and David A Shapiro's book, *Repacking your Bags: How to Live with a New Sense of Purpose,* talks about the process of releasing the old to create space for the new as a passage humans go through, especially when we are going through transitions in our lives. Crises exacerbate the need to look at what we've been doing or carrying in order to make conscious and thoughtful decisions about what we will bring with us as we continue to move forward. For Leider and Shapiro, unpacking refers to "taking a long hard look at what we're carrying and why" (p. vii). For a significant number of people in the middle of a crisis, what they are bringing with them includes a long-overstuffed bag of "shoulds." The shoulds are those behaviors, activities, and beliefs we have collected in our lives, based on our earlier life experiences. And, because we can believe failing to live up to those shoulds will cause us to be harshly judged or rejected by others, we may find ourselves struggling to fulfill them, despite our personal gas tanks being on empty. Creating a new normal in your life is a perfect time to look carefully at the pros and cons of keeping certain shoulds in your life.

Crises, unfortunately, also force us to recognize parts of our past no longer fit our current lives. It's like putting on a pair of jeans which no longer fit, due to changes in your body shape. You might be able to wear them, but it will be uncomfortable or unflattering. Losses can be temporary or permanent—sometimes only time will tell. Trying to make it work when it no longer does will be an energy drain for you.

STRATEGIES

STRATEGY #1. LOOK AT WHAT YOU ARE CARRY-ING.

When my brothers went off to college, leaving only one chick (me) in the nest to cook dinner for, my mother gleefully released the long-held belief she was responsible for ensuring a well-balanced, home-cooked dinner was on the table every night for the family. Instead, we explored restaurants, made our own dinners, and tried out new and different recipes not part of her earlier recipe repertoire. As she let go of her old routine, she inadvertently fostered my culinary interests, creating a love of new cuisines which continues to enhance my life today.

In order to release the obligations or the expectations no longer possible or essential, you have to first name them. Ask yourself the following questions and pay attention what comes up for you:

- What do you believe you should be doing right now you can't seem to make happen? Is it exercising, returning phone calls the same day, cleaning the house, keeping up on Facebook?

- What is missing from your pre-crisis life? What did you do before you are not doing now? How much do you miss it?

- What do you believe your life "should" look like? What standards are you holding yourself to (or assume others are holding you to) which are currently not being met due to this crisis? Alice Domar, Ph.D. and Henry Dreher, in their book *Self-Nurture: Learning to Care for Yourself as Effectively as*

You Care for Everyone Else, notes that while these standards (or, they would suggest, judgments) could be mistaken for rational, appropriate thinking, they are "harsh rebukes of any rising impulse to treat ourselves with tenderness" (p. 13). I notice the effect of these critical voices in the clients I see in my practice. Stressed out and exhausted from their jobs and the needs of their families, they balk at the smallest suggestion it might be okay to hire someone to clean their house, pick up their child from school, or mow the lawn. Somehow, to them, spending money to pay others to do their "job" seems like a dereliction of duty.

- What are your daily and weekly routines? Are you holding onto something taking more energy from you than it provides? For example, is the Thursday evening girls'-night-out bringing fun and relaxation into your life or has it begun to feel like a duty to be squeezed in amongst other, higher-priority responsibilities? Do you find yourself restless and preoccupied while watching the nightly news with your wife every night, as you have for the last fifteen years? Routines can be helpful in a crisis to ground us when much seems upside-down, but they can also deplete our energy. A quick examination of your routines may yield some activities which will serve you best by being released.

Once you've named your shoulds, beliefs, and routines, take a critical look at them. How important are they to your life right now? How feasible or practical are they? Are they worth the energy and time you have to devote to them? Shift your expectations to what will help you manage your life to where you are now, not where you were before the crisis hit, and give yourself permission to change your mind. You are not the person now who created those shoulds back then. You get to decide if they still fit in your life.

STRATEGY #2. WRITE YOUR PATH FORWARD.

I've never been as eloquent in person as I am with the written word. Perhaps it is because on paper I am more open and receptive to hearing something beyond my own voice—Divine nudging or inspiration. During those challenging years, where emotions and personal growth reached new levels, writing became a form of life-support for me. Somehow putting events and emotions on paper helped me find my way back to my own core.

Researchers have been actively exploring the link between writing about emotional topics and positive physical or emotional outcomes for over twenty-five years. The research outcomes have been fairly consistent. A meta-analysis (a study in which numerous separate studies are compared and contrasted in order to extract trends or patterns across all of them) done by J.M Smyth found when subjects wrote about emotional topics they experienced a reduction in distress associated with writing.[17] In addition, multiple other studies found there were positive physical changes, a reduction in physician visits, and less negative emotional distress. Smyth's study also suggested writing over a longer period of time had more positive or long-lasting benefits. Dr. James Pennebaker, author of several books on using expressive writing to facilitate the processing of emotional distress (see Resources), believes when an emotional event occurs, our brains are constantly trying to make sense of it. Once we start translating the distress into words, we make what has happened to us easier to comprehend. Pennebaker also found writers who included more positive, causal, or insight words had improved health. Practically, this suggests, at least to me, finding and expressing both the good in a distressing event, understanding at least some part of why the crisis occurred, and gleaning some insight from a crisis can be beneficial.

- Keep a journal or small laptop with you for the times in the day where waiting intersects with a need or desire to capture what is going on in your internal or external world.

- Use personal blogs, email lists, or other ways (as outlined above in the section on "social media") to allow people to "drop in" on you when they have time. It allows them to keep up with you and your life.

- Take a look at Pennebaker's website (www.writingtoheal.com) for more information and suggestions.

STRATEGY #3. ACCEPT NECESSARY LOSSES ALONG THE WAY.

A crisis can also rip away some of our mainstays—those rituals or repeating events which provide some structure in our lives. Usually, we try particularly hard to find ways to continue those rituals, feeling desperate to hold onto the things that were part of the "old" normal. Yet sometimes they are no longer possible or the cost of continuing those rituals is too dear for us to pay when our energy is being drained by the logistics, decisions, and emotions of the crisis. Rather than spending time and energy trying to force an old pattern into the new space your life currently exists within, let it go.

As you consider your life today, be willing to identify areas where you have been holding on to something your life can no longer easily accommodate. And when you find those shoulds, routines, or expectations in your life that don't make sense right now:

- Be willing to let go of what is no longer working. Figure out what the habit or routine was giving you—a sense of connection, something to count on, a needed break? If it is important, find other ways to get what you need. During Nick's initial stages of chemotherapy our family's twenty-plus-year Friday night pizza routine was not feasible, given Nick's frequent hospital stays. Instead, pizza night occurred whenever possible on the 10th floor of the Children's Medical Center with Nick in bed and friends scattered around the room, eating pizza and playing video games.

- Pay attention to how much time you spend talking about the changes in your life. Track if those conversations make you feel better or worse. If you feel worse after verbally process-ing the numerous ways in which your life has changed, con-sider letting go of the need to talk about what you are miss-ing. It won't change the reality, but it might help your mood.

- Consider what, if anything, you are gaining through the act of releasing. One of my friends, an exceptional and extraor-dinarily hardworking psychologist, discovered after cancer, her energy was no longer the same. Although she worked diligently at regaining it, she never could quite recapture the resilience she had been able to count on over the last thirty-five years of her career. Slowly, she was able to let go of her expectation of returning to her previous self's energy level and found—to her delight—releasing her self-imposed, slightly over-the-top work ethic left more precious time for her family and vacations by the sea.

Judith Viorst, author of *Necessary Losses: The Loves, Illusions, De-pendencies, and Impossible Expectations That All of Us Have to Give Up in Order to Grow*, speaks eloquently of the losses and gains life brings to each one of us. She says, "Making our way from birth to death, we also have to make our way through the pain of giving up and giving up and giving up some portion of what we cherish. We have to deal with our necessary losses. We should un-derstand how these losses are linked to our gains" (p. 366). The gains, such as throwing out outmoded beliefs and expectations, or more precious time to devote to what truly matters and is achiev-able, can be significant.

CHAPTER 2:
DESIGN A BIG ROCK LIFE

Nobody's life is ever all balanced. It's a conscious de-
cision to choose your priorities every day.
–Elisabeth Hasselbeck

Stephen Covey, in his book *The Seven Habits of Highly Effective People,* uses an excellent tool for describing how one lives his/her life with intention—putting the important parts of one's life first. He asks the reader to imagine arranging some large and small rocks, several handfuls of pebbles, and a carton of sand into a container. Generally, people tend to put the sand and pebbles in first, only to find the large rocks won't fit. The only way to fit all of the items— sand, pebbles, and rocks—into the container is to put the large rocks in first, then the small rocks, then the pebbles, and then the sand. Covey uses the large rocks to point to our highest priorities in life. The rest of the materials are those things in our lives—tasks of daily living, challenges of our jobs, maintenance of our lives— which have to be done. If we don't put the large rocks first into our lives, we will never be able to fit them in.

Living with the new normal a crisis brings requires a similar focus: identifying our largest priorities and focusing on them first. Then we can fit in the other necessary aspects of our lives around those priorities. It's a wonderful way to maintain our balance, our intention, and our sanity.

STRATEGIES

STRATEGY #1. PUT YOUR PRIORITIES FIRST.

As you make it through this crisis, what is important to you? If you thought about this at the beginning of the crisis, have those things changed or been modified in any way? Now that you have experienced what it takes to get through the day-to-day living of this new normal, what has to come first? For me, once Vito was out of the hospital and Nick on the road to recovery, one of my biggest priorities was getting regular exercise. For me, getting to the gym at least three days a week was the difference between getting sick from the stress and exhaustion and having the stamina to be the caregiver my family needed. It was one of my big rocks, as important to me as being there for Vito and Nick, maintaining a close connection to family, friends, and the Divine, staying positive and grateful, and showing up for my clients. Here's a method to help you do that:

- *Step one*: Make public your priorities—Let people hear what you have to put first in your life right now. Develop an elevator speech (a one-to-two-minute explanation of the crisis and the changes it has made in your priorities). For example, Heather, a client who was going through a divorce, wrote an email with her husband to explain to friends and family how they were planning to handle their divorce. They wanted their community of support to understand the divorce would be cordial and keeping their three children whole through the process was the couple's highest priority. Once you decide how public you want to make your priorities, some options for doing so include: telling friends over dinner, sending an email to the family, having a meeting with your direct reports at work, or asking a "connector" in your life to take on the role of communicator. As was mentioned in the previous stage, social media would probably not be the best forum for this kind of communication.

- *Step two*: Get creative with your obligations—Recognize what must be done that doesn't come easily to you or takes energy from you. It will still have to be done, so why not try to figure out a system to make it easier or at least more enjoyable? For example, a crisis can bring mounds of paperwork and bills, something I can handle capably but dislike doing. While Vito, the family administrator, was in the hospital and I was responsible for paying bills (something I can do capably but dislike intensely) I discovered a chilled glass of Kali Hart chardonnay was the best way to bribe myself into bill-paying activity. A few suggestions:

  o Make the duty more pleasurable by pairing it with something you like to do. For me, a glass of wine was more pleasurable than paying bills! Yours might be a piece of chocolate, watching TV, reading a book, or talking on the phone. The idea is to use something to reward yourself for doing the necessary but unpleasant or draining task.

  o Get inventive—what would make it fun? Brainstorm with a friend different ways to accomplish the task.

  o Try parallel play. I can get significantly more done if I am working alongside someone else. Try enlisting a friend who has a similarly burdensome task needing to be done and work on your tasks together.

  o If possible, pay someone to take it off your hands.

STRATEGY #2. SET BOUNDARIES.

For the easily distracted and exhausted people-pleasers, setting boundaries falls under the category of "easier said than done." Nevertheless, it is a key factor in making it through the crisis; without boundaries, the intentions can't be put into practice. A few ideas to help you set some limits in your life are:

- *Step one*: Start small—Pick one or two areas of your life where saying no seems relatively low-risk and/or painless. If you are badly out of practice, start with telephone solicitors. Pick up the phone when they call and say, "Thank you for calling. My family/I am going through a crisis right now and I don't have the time or space to listen to your offer. Have a great day." Then hang up. Did you tell them more information than they needed? You bet. But you were able to practice on someone whom you will never meet and you did it politely.

- *Step two:* Become your own bouncer—We were extraordinarily lucky with the support system we had surrounding us during those years. Yet accepting the loving offers of assistance while balancing what was truly helpful to our family required thought and tact. Those qualities are, at least for me, inversely correlated with fatigue. I had to learn to rely on my gut. When someone asked how they could be helpful or if they could come by, I took a moment to check in with my body. Did it feel lighter in response to the query? Or, did something twist and a sense of dread or guilt come over me? Those were my signs the thoughtful and kind offer being made would not be helpful to me. If I listened to my body, it was a reliable indicator of where an energy boundary needed to be set. The process of listening to my own inner wisdom and acting on it meant using some poorly developed muscles. The dividends associated with strengthening those muscles were tremendous, both then and now.

- *Step three:* Differentiate between "kind" and "nice"—A good friend of mine who seems to have little difficulty saying no once told me there is a difference between being kind and being nice. As we talked about the two concepts, it became clear to me that kindness—a thoughtful, compassionate, honest approach to another human being—was completely in keeping with my values. Niceness depended on me ascertaining and responding to other people's wants – despite the fact it meant denying my own needs or truth. For example, spending time on the phone with a friend who only wants to fill time before her husband comes home from work would be "nice." Yet, given the myriad of responsibilities I had to accomplish during a day, it meant staying up later than planned, or giving up some of my time to accommodate her desire. Taking some time to be with a friend or client who is struggling with a decision or life event was typically an act of kindness. If it was important and I could be helpful, without causing undue strain for myself, I would step in. The difference was the kind offer came from a deeply genuine part of me, rather than in reaction to a social convention or early training. In short, I found being kind is profoundly important to me while being nice generally seems to take me further and further away from my priorities.

- *Step four:* Create reminders to help you focus—As someone who suffers from the DEBSO syndrome (Distracted Easily by Shiny Objects), I need all the help I can get to remain clear about what I am putting first in my life. My intentions are consistently good, but without daily reminders and rituals to keep me on track, I find myself in front of the computer playing Tetris. Some ideas might be:

    o Find a quote or affirmation to summarize your top priorities. Affirmations have been shown to have a buffering effect in stressful situations in several research studies, improving problem-solving,[18] reducing negative or depressive thoughts and enhancing positive psychological and physical outcomes.[19] Particularly useful are those affirmations incorporating your personal values and strengths. For example, if one of your top priorities is eating healthy, an affirmation might be, "I consistently choose the most nutritious options for my body. I listen to what my body needs for its optimum health."

○ Enlist technology. Set a priorities reminder on your phone. In simple, affirmative phrasing, write down how you choose to organize your day. For example, "I exercise every morning and eat a good breakfast to make sure my body is ready for the day."

As Steven Covey says, "The key is not to prioritize what is on your schedule, but to schedule your priorities." A crisis is both the best excuse and most compelling reason I have encountered to make different choices than you have in the past. That being said, a new choice is only as effective as the support you give it. If you can breathe life into your priorities through personal accountability and new behaviors, they can accompany you on the rest of the journey and beyond the end of the current crisis. Mine did.

STRATEGY #3. LET THE UNIVERSE AFFIRM YOU.

I believe the Universe (God, Allah, the Divine) and the souls which are part of its vast and loving nature are ever-present in our lives—providing support and guidance to us. We are the ones who are oblivious to the assistance we are being offered in symbols, synchronicity, and miracles. One particularly meaningful symbol of encouragement for me—especially whenever I am dealing with a new normal in my life—is feathers. There is a Native American belief that finding a feather directly in front of you means you are on your path—your actions are in alignment with your Divine spirit. More times than I can count, during those three years and afterwards, I would look down and find a feather on my path—usually when I desperately needed the encouragement to remind me I was not alone, the Universe was with me on this journey, I was doing something right, and I was loved.

Marci Shimoff, author of *Happy for No Reason: 7 Steps to Being Happy From the Inside Out* and the *Chicken Soup for the Soul* series, talks about the incredible number of people who have sent her stories about the signs they had received (for example, bluebirds and cardinals show up repeatedly), in response to prayer or other need. She suggests signs are one of the ways we can listen to the wisdom within us connected to the Divine.

- Be open to the possibility the Divine, in whatever way you imagine it, is sending you messages of encouragement and love.

- Pay attention to things occurring around you repeatedly, when they occur, and the conditions under which they show up in your life.

If there is a pattern, decide what it means to you and if it feels encouraging, integrate it into your life by noticing it, journaling about it, or giving thanks when it occurs. Everyone needs positive reinforcement, especially in crisis. Open up to the possibility that the encouragement and reinforcement your soul needs as you traverse the crisis can come in unusual and unlikely ways.

CHAPTER 3:
PUT ON YOUR OXYGEN MASK FIRST

In dealing with those who are undergoing great suffering, if you feel "burnout" setting in, if you feel demoralized and exhausted, it is best, for the sake of everyone, to withdraw and restore yourself. The point is to have a long-term perspective.
–Dalai Lama

There is a reason that flight attendants on every flight remind parents and those traveling with people who need their help to first put on their own oxygen masks should cabin pressure drop. If the caretakers have passed out, they can't render care. The new "normal" a crisis brings requires we stay balanced, healthy, and relatively sane. This means finding ways to handle our emotions, maintain our physical health, and keep ourselves on an even keel. Doing so is difficult, indeed counterintuitive with the sense of urgency a crisis perpetuates in our lives. Taking care of yourself in the middle of a crisis, especially if it involves your loved ones, can feel like an act of selfishness. How can we take time away from them or from their crises to renew ourselves? We become engaged in the crisis to the point of superstition—afraid a single moment of distraction will result in additional disaster. When a loved one is in crisis, an unremitting focus on his needs seems the only way we can balance out the unfairness of the situation.

It requires a long-term perspective, as the Dalai Lama points out, to envision giving yourself permission to tend to your own needs. Rarely do those going through crises understand at the beginning the importance of their self-care to providing continuing assistance or to staying capable. Medical staff can also be trapped by the same sense of guilt. A friend of mine, a pediatric oncologist, once shared how difficult the decision was to go home to his family when one of his patients was dying. It seems almost like an abandonment of both the patient and the family in their worst time. How could the needs of his son, a normal, healthy child, compare to theirs?

The importance of self-care is not immediately apparent—especially to those of us who are used to running on empty in the service of others. It is only after some weeks or months have passed, when you begin to feel the impact of the late nights, bad food, and constant stress when it becomes clear the energy required to provide effective handling of the crisis also requires self-nurturing. When it becomes clear this crisis will not quickly leave the stage, or an immediate resolution is not forthcoming, this radical idea begins to make sense. When you are supported, and your needs are met, you are more powerful and more effective at doing what needs to be done.

STRATEGIES

STRATEGY #1. FIRE YOUR INNER SUPERHERO.

Admitting you can't do everything yourself is wisdom, not weakness. One of the chapters in Brené Brown's wonderful book, *The Gifts of Imperfection: Let Go of Who You Think You're Supposed to Be to Embrace Who You Are*, says it well. (*Guidepost #7: Cultivating Play and Rest: Letting Go of Exhaustion as a Status Symbol and Productivity as Self-Worth*) Brené talks about how we equate self-worth with our ability to churn out work, making the idea of rest, much less play, a form of unacceptable mutiny in our minds. Yet Dr. Brown also cites research and findings in multiple scientific disciplines which recognize the importance of play to *our ability to be productive* [Italics added]. Our tendency to over-function can be hidden best from ourselves. Explore how you might be unknowingly channeling your inner superhero by considering these:

- Do any of these "larger-than-life" stories sound like you? Superwoman, Rescuer, People pleaser, Problem solver, Steady one, Rock, Nurturer, or Helper.

- If not, consider the role you typically take on when there is a crisis in your family or among your close friends. What do people call you for? Help? Advice? Money? Someone to fix things?

- Reflect on the implications of this story during this crisis. Where will it help you and where will it hurt you?

Inner superheroes take various forms and, although they don't unfailingly wear a cape, they can be identified by their propensity to take on too much and/or be in charge. The clients I work with in my therapy practice are usually highly competent, take-charge people with excellent problem-solving abilities. Frequently, they come from families where those skills are in short supply, leaving them in charge whenever a family crisis occurs. Those same talents, unfortunately, make it excessively difficult for them when the crisis falls in their own front yard. One of my clients, an eminently successful accountant in her forties, found it hard to tell her husband she needed his help in overcoming her desire to numb her anxiety with pain-killers. She was used to his admiration for her competence and becoming vulnerable enough to share her pain took tremendous courage. Ultimately, it was a turning point for the marriage. After all, superheroes can be hard to live with sometimes!

STRATEGY #2. TUNE INTO YOUR NEEDS.

Similar to when you set an intention of who and how you would be during the crisis (Regain Your Balance), nurturing yourself is a choice. Unfortunately, it's not an obvious one (especially for those of us with superhero tendencies), but it is a vital decision. When taking care of yourself becomes one of the "big rocks" in your life, it begins to be part of your day-to-day plan of action.

- *Step one:* Plan ahead—In crisis, self-nurture is extremely critical but takes some strategizing to pull off. The minute you recognize this crisis is expected to be a long-term situation, create the space in your schedule to take care of yourself.

  - People in crisis often decide to wait until things seem less hectic or less critical to schedule their self-care. There certainly are times when being present is imperative, but they are less frequent than one would imagine. With cell phones and the Internet, we are rarely completely out of touch with one another. Making time to take care of yourself requires four important steps: 1) schedule it and notify people you will not be available; 2) work out a plan to have your presence covered, if necessary; 3) make sure people are aware of how to reach you and the circumstances under which you want to be contacted; and 4) *take* the time.

o   If the crisis involves taking care of a loved one who can participate in a conversation, talk to him or her about your needs during this crisis. "I am committed to you and helping you through this time. I suspect there will be long nights/considerable stress/an emotional roller coaster as we go through this together. To keep myself healthy, I am going to need some time away/by myself on a regular basis. Let's figure out how to make it happen with minimal disruption."

o   If the crisis involves someone who can't participate in the conversation, engage a friend or loved one to help you brainstorm ways to carve out regular amounts of time where you can renew and self-nurture. I have sent countless clients home with the assignment to contact their best friends or closest family members in order to "think through the possibilities." Invariably they return with an action plan to enlist a family member's help or a new resource to provide them with the break they have desperately needed but wouldn't take. Somehow, having the permission of others to take a break was the push they required.

• *Step two*: Take stock—One of the first steps in recognizing you are in need of self-care is paying attention to the status of your entire self.

○ *Physically*. As I pointed out in "Survive the Initial Shock", during a crisis, our minds are typically so busy with the logistics and fears our bodies' needs go unnoticed. As the crisis continues, it remains critical you check in regularly to find out what your body is telling you. Pay attention to the mundane (hungry, thirsty, exhausted) as well as the more serious (unusual pains, breathing problems, or digestive reactions). Stress takes a huge toll on the body over time and paying attention to symptoms when they arise helps you stay healthy.

   • *Body Scan*. Sitting in a still but comfortable position, begin to breathe deeply and slowly. Breathe in to the count of five (or more if you can), then breathe out for one more count than you breathed in. Starting at the top of your head (keep breathing), tune in to each part of your body (head, chest, back, arms, hands, abdomen, hips, legs, and feet). Pay attention to where you feel discomfort (tightness, pain, pinching) and where you feel relaxed. Then gauge your level of tiredness or hunger. Make a note of where the problems are.

○ *Emotionally*. Many of us were taught as children to ignore or repress our emotions because our parents were never taught how to manage their own reactions, much less ours. As a result, we learned to stuff them, mislabel them ('I'm not angry, I'm concerned"), or rationalize them ("I shouldn't be hurt; she didn't mean anything by her comment"). In a crisis, the ability to recognize, feel, and allow an emotion to emerge in a safe way can make the difference between total burnout or resentment and staying present and whole. But first, we have to learn how to truly recognize and feel an emotion.

- *Emotional Scan.* Continuing to breathe, put your hand over your heart and sit quietly. Every time a thought comes to you, release it as you would a butterfly from your hand, seeing it move away from you. Slowly, you may begin to feel some emotions. Note them and then release them—don't spend any time trying to figure them out. After about five minutes, take out a piece of paper and write down the emotions you were feeling.

○ *Mentally.* Author Michael Singer, in *The Untethered Soul,* notes the tremendous drain on our energy our thoughts and emotions can have. He enumerates the ways we can deplete ourselves, simply by thinking: "Creating thoughts, holding onto thoughts, recalling thoughts, generating emotions, controlling emotions, and disciplining powerful inlet drives, all require a tremendous expenditure of energy." Nurturing yourself can mean watching your thoughts like you pay attention to your body—alert to signs mental exhaustion may be looming.

- *Mind Scan.* For a couple of days, keep a small notebook and jot down the recurring thoughts coming to you. If you recognize the emotion accompanying with the thought, write it down as well. For example: Monday a.m.—found myself fearful about what the CT scans would show.
Monday a.m.—was obsessing over doctor's comment about Nick's counts—anxiety high.
Monday p.m.—worried about getting report to client on time.

Monday, middle of the night—woke up and started worrying about how to handle the insurance stuff.

- At the end of those days, notice any recurring themes. These are where your mind monkeys like to take you when you're not paying attention. Use these themes as warning signals to take action in some way—set a boundary, take better care of yourself and your spirit.

STRATEGY #3. HANDLE (YOURSELF) WITH CARE.

Now that you are aware of what your body is experiencing and what you are feeling, give some thought to what will help. Physically, you may benefit from a massage, better food, exercise, deep breathing, or perhaps a doctor's visit. Emotionally, you may need a safe way to express your anger or frustration. The scan may reveal to you you don't feel heard, or you need a witness to your tears or sadness. Whatever it is, knowing where you are gives you a place from which to begin.

- *Step one*: Find people or activities to energize you—We are told as children we can't "go play" until we have done our chores. Most crises (and, in some ways, our adult roles) come with such an endless list of "chores" we can never completely finish. Play is creative and it renews our energy. It also reminds us we are so much more than the tasks in front of us. Some ways of including more play into your life could include:

  ○ Schedule an afternoon or morning to go on your own adventure. Do something to revive those aspects of you which have taken a back seat to the process of getting through the crisis. Be sure it's something that will leave you more optimistic, energized, or upbeat than you were when you started.

- o Julia Cameron's *The Artist's Way* gives the assignment of taking "artist's dates" once a week to rekindle the creative part of you. Cameron describes the artist date as a "once-weekly, festive, solo expedition to explore something intriguing or interesting to you... Artist Dates fire up the imagination. They spark whimsy. They encourage play...They feed our creative work by replenishing our inner well of images and inspiration.[20] " If only for an hour once a week, take yourself on a date. It can be to a museum, a book store, a fly fishing shop, a motorcycle showroom, or a unique store. Pick somewhere you've never been before and go explore.

- o Enlist a friend who knows what will energize you to entice you to "come out and play" on a regular basis.

- *Step two*: Look for what soothes you—Self-nurturing involves understanding what is nurturing or soothing to you. If this concept is new to you, here are some questions to start you on the right path towards discovering the answer:

  - o What activities have relaxed you in the past? This can include physical activities such as spin class, tennis, or golf. It can also include pampering like massages, hot baths, getting a manicure or pedicure. One of my clients, when pushed to come up with at least one suggestion to provide a break in his hectic, workaholic career, remembered the joy and relaxation he felt as a young teen, hunting with his dog. As we plundered his memory for stress-relieving ideas, he was able to reengage with a love of the outdoors he had lost amidst the shuffle of work papers. Slowly, starting with walks around his neighborhood, we rekindled his connection with Nature, providing him some much-needed relief from an overly ambitious workday.

o   Are there people in your life who make you feel cared for when you are around them? What about a girls'/guys' night out?

o   What are the foods you remember loving in your childhood? Macaroni and cheese? Peanut butter sandwiches? Typically, people find carbohydrates or creamy textures soothing (If you are under dietary restrictions, consider consulting a nutritionist to find options that work for you).

o   Which kinds of pictures create a feeling of calm for you? Mountains? The ocean? Flowers? Children laughing? Foreign lands? Searching through picture albums, the Internet, or magazines can yield a surprising number of options.

Once you've identified what kinds of things soothe you, create ways to bring them into your life on a regular basis. Enlist caring family and friends to help you find opportunities to weave these forms of self-nurture into your day-to-day activities.

STRATEGY #4. HONOR YOUR EMOTIONS AND YOUR ENERGY.

Compartmentalization has consistently been one of my favorite coping mechanisms. For someone who is not organized by nature, the idea of tucking away a concern or fear into a small box to be opened later was curiously appealing. I had learned to use compartmentalization during my graduate school years when I was juggling motherhood, marriage, and a Ph.D. program, but Nick's and Vito's illnesses made me a pro at the skill.

During a crisis, it's critical to your health and your psychological state of being to allow yourself the space and time for tears, anxiety, fear, or other negative emotions. Research suggests failure to process emotional events can leave you in a state of emotional arousal which generates increased anxiety, leads to depression, strains your cardiovascular system, and can result in a less efficient immune system.[21] As a therapist, I can add stuffing emotions, rather than honoring them at the time, is ineffective—they will show up, one day, cleverly disguised as something else and triggered by what appears to be at the time an unconnected event.

As with suppressing emotions, perfectionism also drains our energy. Brené Brown finds, based on her research, everyone lives somewhere on the perfectionism scale. Those of us who tend to hang out on the high end can frequently fall prey to believing we must handle everything perfectly every single time. She says, "Perfectionism is self-destructive because there is no such thing as perfect. Perfectionism is an unattainable goal." (p. 57)[22] You have a tremendous amount of stuff going on. Don't expect yourself to handle things perfectly all the time. Forgive yourself when you don't.

Sometimes what is draining you is not the situation or your own desire to do things perfectly—people and their conscious or unconscious neediness can deplete our energy without us knowing it. A young woman came to me several years ago, trying to make up her mind about a relationship she was in. Clara had been living with her thirty-something boyfriend for several years but couldn't decide whether or not she wanted to marry him. He was getting impatient with her indecisiveness and had suggested therapy. As Clara told me more about her boyfriend, it became obvious (at least to me) their relationship was largely one-sided. She was expected to adapt and adjust her life around his needs, be constantly available to soothe his frequently hurt ego, and take on all of the roles typically associated with a wife.

As she described her relationship with him, I heard nothing about reciprocity—no nurturing of her and her needs. I began to ask questions about how she felt when she was around him and she admitted she was, more times than not, drained by their interactions and was frankly delighted when his business took him out of town. As we continued to explore what she was getting out of the relationship, the unequal equation became acutely apparent to her. Her childhood issues with rejection and abandonment had blinded her to the fact that taking care of him was eating up her time and putting her beginning career as a photographer on hold. She tried to work with him to change the nature of their relationship, asking for her needs to be met, choosing to self-nurture, and working through her fears. When none of those measures worked, Clara decided it was time to let the relationship go.

Judith Orloff, a board-certified psychiatrist, was one of the first medical professionals I read who talks about energy vampires. She uses this term to describe people who leave you fatigued every time you interact with them. Consistently needy or feeling victimized, these energy-depleters find people who are caring, nurturing helpers to befriend. It is rarely a conscious act on the part of the energy vampire. Rather they are feeling so depleted themselves, they seek others to fill them up, instead of looking within for what they need to do to nurture their own happiness.

While most people go through periods of their lives when they're needy or count on the comfort of others, energy vampires are characterized by the unending nature of their need for someone who will help them feel better about themselves. It is important to remember, energy resources can be depleted and replenished. Be thoughtful about what and whom you allow into your life during the crisis. To locate and deal with any potential energy vampires in your life:

- *Step one:* Make a list of the people with whom you interact regularly. Rate how much you look forward to being with them on a scale of 1-10 (1 = not at all, 10 = thrilled and can't wait). Then, using the same rating scale, rate how you feel after being with them (1 = want to crawl in bed and sleep/totally depressed/spitting mad, 10 = loving life and yourself/totally energized).

- *Step two:* Decide if there is a way to limit or eliminate contact with the people who rate on the low end of the scale while you are going through the crisis. This is particularly difficult for my clients who are in a helping profession or in roles requiring them to work extensively with others. Recently I met with a young man who was experiencing both a toxic work environment and some draining work relationships. Together we crafted a plan to increase the number of days he worked at home, as well as utilizing email and Skype to limit the face-to-face contact he had to have with the difficult individuals. During a crisis, you need every crumb of energy you can get. Spending it unconsciously or because of guilt both depletes your stores and does not make a significant long-term difference in the life of the energy vampire.

- *Step three:* Create an emotional shield—Crises can highlight or bring up unresolved issues in families. Emotions can be raw and others may use you, consciously or unconsciously, as a dumping ground for their own fear, anxiety, anger, or grief. If you are sensitive to the emotions of others, it is critical you find a way to separate what others are feeling from what you are experiencing.

    o Find an image of protection appealing to you. I use an oval of shimmering, iridescent light that surrounds my body. Water pours over the oval, flushing away everything draining, causing stress, or terrorizing me. A client of mine found the idea of a suit of mirrors compelling, using it to send back the emotions to the person initiating them. My more Star Trek-oriented clients loved the idea of a force field. And, since mental imagery has been found to be more effective when the other senses are included, feel free to add imagined sounds, smells (such as aromatherapy), and tactile responses to your visualization.

○ Whatever image you use, make it part of your daily habits. Brush your teeth, take your medicine, and put on your shield.

Visualization (or mental imagery, as it is generally referred to) has been used across multiple disciplines for a variety of reasons, from improving athletic performance to speeding healing,[23] alleviating chronic pain,[24] or calming anxiety or fears.[25] Particularly relevant to crises, studies have found the use of positive mental imagery can both decrease negative emotions and increase positive emotions. Taking the research one step further, in the last twenty years healers such as Larry Dossey (*Reinventing Medicine: Beyond the Mind-Body and Into a New Era of Healing*) and others have explored the inter-action between positive mental imagery and physiological or bio-logical responses in another person. Their findings suggest we can not only impact our own physical or mental health through visuali-zation but that of others—a mind-boggling idea.

STRATEGY #5. NURTURE YOUR SPIRIT.

Eighteen months into my family's crises, it felt as if my life was being rewritten into one where the needs of my spirit seemed less and less important. To regain my connection to spirit, I wanted to do some-thing somewhat radical—I decided to enlist the assistance of a medicine woman, a shaman. Shamans have been spiritual leaders for indigenous tribes throughout history. In the modern day world, shamans are frequently Native Americans or others who devote se-rious study to the process of helping others heal by reclaiming the parts of their souls they have lost along the way. A shamanic journey struck me as the right way to retrieve those missing parts of myself while nurturing myself spiritually.

I connected with a woman recommended by several friends whom I trusted and arranged for an appointment one afternoon. The shaman was a pleasant woman in her thirties who met me at the door of her suburban home and explained what the ceremony would entail. For the next hour, in a room filled with sacred symbols and tobacco smoke (part of the process), I had a full-body shamanic experience. I was chanted over, brushed with rabbit fur, and prayed over. I moved into a light trance and abandoned myself to the experience.

As part of the debrief, the shaman shared some visions she had received about my life—they had mostly to do with allowing myself to be the healer I was here to be. Most of what I took away from my afternoon escape was a sense of renewal. In the middle of the sterile, medical world I was living in, the brief holiday into the land of Native American mysticism had been water to my parched spirit.

Crises take so much from us—mentally, physically, and emotionally—it is easy to forget the impact it can have on your spirit, your sense of connection to love, wonder, nature or whatever Spirit means to you. Part of staying whole is tending to the condition of your spirit as thoughtfully as you tend to your other needs.

- The new normal may be a temporary way station on your path to crisis resolution or it may be a more permanent way of living. Nothing, not even this new normal, lasts forever. Regardless of how long you find yourself in this new place, the process of re-evaluation and release will provide you with the space to maneuver. Self-care—the other half of the equation in making the new normal work—is a radical concept for a significant number of people, especially for those of us who love to help others. It is a bit of a circular process—valuing yourself enough to ask for what you need creates in turn a sense of self-worth. But wherever you start in the journey—taking care of your emotions, your body, your spirit or your mind and in whatever ways make sense to you—please make the intention to do so. It will provide you with the energy to cope with the requirements of the space you are in.

THE FIFTH STAGE:
RE-EMERGE AND TAKE FLIGHT

*I can be changed by what happens to me. But I refuse
to be reduced by it.*
–Maya Angelou

Butterflies have an innate sense informing them when to emerge from the cocoon. Perhaps it is a set number of days, or the right amount of warmth striking their cocoons. Whatever the signal, it is a lesson in patience to watch a butterfly break free of the cocoon that has hidden its transformation. The butterfly comes out of its previous home excruciatingly slowly, pausing repeatedly to rest and recover from the exertion. Even after it has pulled itself fully from the cocoon, the butterfly clings to it, tentatively flexing its wings, waiting for them to dry before attempting the first flight. Finally, the wings send a signal they are ready to support the weight of its previously earthbound body and the butterfly takes flight—to the closest source of nourishment. There, amidst the blossoms of the neighboring plants, the butterfly breaks its long fast, gathering strength for its new life. The butterfly instinctively knows what it needs for the journey into the new world of beauty and flight.

There is a cocoon element to crisis. We hunker down, burying ourselves in the warm embrace of friends, or isolating ourselves and our feelings in order to soldier through the innumerable challenges crisis brings to us. Our cocoon can become familiar to us—perhaps we have learned the limits of what we are capable during those strenuous times. Some uncover reserves of courage and strength previously unseen. Others come up against an uncrossable boundary leading to a bone-deep unwillingness to be held responsible anymore for another's unhappiness, addictions, or choices. If we are lucky, we have been forgiven much by our employers, family, and friends as we grappled with the changes in our lives. With the world held at least partially at bay during the worst of the crisis, we can become our own world, wrapped up into the all-consuming logistics of traversing the difficult, and sometimes terrifying, terrain to which our challenges have brought us.

Once the crisis has abated, we are tempted to try to put everything behind us and forge quickly ahead, wanting to recapture the time seemingly lost. Yet, allowing ourselves to be transformed by the crisis requires the same patience as the process of metamorphosing from a caterpillar into a butterfly. The darkness and the drain of the cocoon must first be replenished. We are not immediately ready to return to the tempo of our pre-crisis lives. Perhaps we are not sure of what is the same and what has irrevocably changed.

It can be difficult to discern or articulate the ways in which we have changed and then to decide what to do with those modifications to our sense of self. It takes time to recover, usually more time than we expect. And it takes some distance from the crisis, as well as observation, reflection, and action, to allow ourselves to fully understand not only how but also the extent to which we have been transformed. In fact, I was surprised how frequently, in my interviews for *The Wisdom of Cancer,* my interviewees expressed gratitude for the reflection our conversations spurred in their lives. Stopping their busy lives to talk again about their crisis, they were able to recognize more clearly their path and the ways in which their experience with cancer had changed them.

Looking out of the rearview mirror has had a similar benefit in my life. As I study the path I have been on, I notice the uneven traces of my journey. Some steps were slow and measured. There were also traces of great leaps forward. But, when I look backwards and reflect, I perceive the absolute rightness of my progress. I recognize what I thought I wanted (a mate, a job, a trip) at each point in the journey would not have served me well. Each time I view my path from the perspective of where I am now, I find myself releasing a bit more of my need to control what is in front of me. As I relax a fraction more into the peace that is surrender, it helps me hear the rhythm of transformation.

CHAPTER 1:
RE-EMERGE FROM YOUR CRISIS

*The further you are challenged and threatened, the
more your warrior heart will emerge.*
–Bryant McGill

The end of a crisis, trauma, or serious illness can engender both excitement and anxiety. Particularly with a crisis that has, at least on the face of it, an ending point-such as a divorce granted, discharge from rehab, release from treatment for a serious illness. It can be unnerving to be faced with a punctuation point.

People report a sense of disorientation or loss, even an unwillingness or hesitancy to believe the crisis has come to an end. When Nick was told by his oncologist at Children's Medical Center, "We mean this in the nicest possible way but we hope to never see you again," it was thrilling and also felt the tiniest bit like abandonment. These people who had consistently been there for the last three years of our lives, at the other end of the phone or in a hospital room, whenever a cancer-related problem arose, were telling us we no longer belonged. Nick had similar feelings. It was hard for him to believe he was through—he asked for a CT scan, to make sure.

And while the crisis may have ended, not infrequently there are lingering physical reactions or issues—fatigue, anxiety, secondary illness caused or resulting from the original crisis. Survivors of extreme trauma may find themselves experiencing signs of post-traumatic stress disorder such as intensive and pervasive flashbacks, intrusive thoughts, or feeling emotionally numb.

The amount of support people get when they are emerging from a crisis also varies widely—depending on the crisis and those involved with helping the person through the crisis. Clients have shared with me the divorce parties they have had, or the homecomings they have received. The residential treatment center where Nick now works with adolescents who have experienced serious family, legal, and school issues due to their behavior choices understands the importance of this process. When a young person has been deemed ready to leave, his treatment team and family meet to discuss what he or she has learned: coping skills, triggers, and stressors. The departing resident is given advice by his or her peers about strengths and continued areas for development. Along with staff from the unit, the young person takes a trial run back out in the world—going for a movie and dinner, or some other "normal" activity. Then finally, when the resident is ready to graduate, he or she takes the "eagle's flight," jumping off of a platform (safely secured in harness), into a designated sacred space. There the graduate is given a totem animal for guidance and protection on the journey ahead.

For most of us, though, the process of emerging is less well-attended or well-thought-out. We are aware of our family and friends' desire for our lives to "go back to normal." We must listen to our own hearts about what we need as we move tentatively into this space of "after." Reflecting, honoring our experiences and our bodies—moving slowly forward will serve us well.

STRATEGIES

STRATEGY #1. RECOGNIZE AND ACCEPT THE END-INGS.

One morning in the September before Vito died, as I sat writing in my leather-bound diary, the image of a roller-coaster came to me. What our family had experienced over the last three years had had its terrifying twists, turns, and plunges. As I reflected further, a roller-coaster ride also seemed the perfect metaphor for life. We all have our roller-coasters—marital difficulties, financial problems, medical issues, and self-esteem and relationship problems. I've learned it's not about waiting for the roller-coaster to stop or resigning oneself to the rickety, swaying motion of the seat. It's about integrating the movement—the highs, lows, twists, and straight paths—into your perspective of what life is. There were important questions I had had to ask myself during this ride that had been our family's journey since October 2005. Were we spending our time facing backwards, talking to everyone about how frightening the last turn was? Were we worrying about when the next big drop will come—craning our necks and squirming in our seats to see if it is immediately ahead of us? Did we have our eyes shut, so we didn't have to take in all the possibilities of what might happen on the ride, at least not all at once? Were we holding on for dear life, waiting for the ride to end? Were we clutching the person next to us fearfully, hoping he or she would somehow keep us safe? Or were we sitting with friends, seat belts firmly fastened, with our hands in the air, open to the possibilities, trusting the ride's designer? I had fallen into each of those categories in a given month, week, or day.

Elizabeth Kubler-Ross, psychiatrist and pioneer in researching the process of death and dying, elucidated a five-stage model of grief her patients seemed to pass through when facing their death or the death of a loved one.[26] While she did not believe everyone goes through the same stages or that the stages were necessarily linear, her work has been pivotal in understanding how significant changes in individuals' lives are experienced. With the final stage, Acceptance, Kubler-Ross suggests there is a sense of homeostasis and a readiness to move into life as it has become. As you sense a shift towards some kind of closure or ending in the crisis that held you in its grasp up until now, it may be helpful to ask yourself:

- Is there an ending approaching?

- Who do you want to be as the ending unfolds? How do you want to act? What qualities and characteristics do you want to demonstrate? How will you do this? Is there someone whom you can recruit or count on who will help you stay true to your intentions?

- What do you need to be ready for this ending? Do you need time alone (journaling, praying, reflecting, reading, or walking in nature) or the support of others (calling in family, gathering trusted friends, connecting with my spiritual community, or seeking expert counsel from a spiritual leader, therapist, doctor, lawyer, or financial adviser)?

- What is important to me right now? To say? To do? To take care of?

Marriages end in various ways—the movement towards divorce can come after a single act of betrayal, years of emotional challenges, threats, and attempts at reconciliation, or perhaps stutter to a stop, no longer fueled by the energy it needs to stay alive. When clients discuss their impending divorces with me I first seek to understand the assorted reasons behind their decision as well as the emotional challenges they are currently facing as they look towards a different and sometimes uncertain future. Fairly quickly, though, I ask about their intentions. There are numerous and complicated emotions swirling around a couple as they divorce: sadness, anger, frustration, shock, resignation, fear. It is easy to be hijacked by the emotions into acting in ways that later cause regret—for example, cutting off from family, or advertising dirty laundry in a desire to vindicate their decision to divorce. I have found asking this single question and helping them craft thoughtful responses provide a place for them to move from, a certainty entirely theirs to control. Regardless of the endings my clients are facing—a custody battle, bankruptcy, or other highly emotional transitions—having a goal to guide them (as they did in the beginning) gives them a way of dealing with the ending consciously and purposefully. I have found doing so typically leads to far fewer struggles down the road or personal ruefulness due to poorly-thought-out reactions or triggers.

STRATEGY #2. CREATE A RITUAL THAT HONORS YOUR JOURNEY.

The process of recognizing the ending of a crisis and finding a path forward happens in a variety of ways. Yet oftentimes my clients report there is no single event to mark the ending, such as a death or having the legal papers signed. Rather, it seems to take the perspective of time to discern the crisis has started its movement toward the past. They recognize the ending by the absence or abatement of racing thoughts, exhaustion, or other mental and physical symptoms associated with the crisis. Some clients notice they have more time to spend on other important matters; their time is no longer as constrained as it was when the crisis was in full swing. Others recognize the ending of the challenging times through their emotions—they are no longer as sad, angry, fearful, or anxious as they were in the earlier days of the crisis. More than one client has talked about a rekindling interest in an important part of their lives rendered dormant while the challenges they were facing consumed all of their waking moments. It is when they come into a session talking about a movie they saw over the weekend, planting their vegetable garden, or travel they are planning which tells me they are beginning to move beyond the crisis.

It is useful, regardless of how the ending arrives, to observe it in some way. There is a reason rituals such as funerals and celebrations have been part of humankind's journey from the beginning. In *Transformative Rituals: Celebrations for Personal Growth*, authors Gay and David Williamson note rituals are a way to recognize the powerful and sacred force within us. They write, "Rituals are a vehicle to help us experience inner and outer transformation...When we pause to find the sacredness in the everyday context of life, we are renewed and transformed." Crises can yield a deep awareness of our own fortitude as well as our vulnerabilities. Recognizing this knowledge throughout the act of creating and enacting a ritual allows us to begin to tell ourselves how this crisis has changed us. We begin to understand better the mark it has made on our lives and perhaps our souls. It is, for a significant number of people, a way to both claim their new identities—as those who have been altered during the challenges they have faced—and to note the beginning of the next phase of their lives.

Therapeutically, rituals have been used for years in numerous ways: to help with the bereavement process, to assist a family in negotiating its way through life-cycle changes or significant events, to provide a safe place for survivors of rape and sexual abuse to tell their stories and reclaim their power, and to signal the healing of an emotional or physical wound such as ceremonies where members of Alcoholics Anonymous receive chips for extended periods of sobriety.

A ritual I suggest to clients who are redefining their identities by moving from one phase of their lives to another—be it a job, a marriage, the ending of a crisis, or perhaps a stage in their lives—is to take out two pieces of paper and record 1) what they are leaving behind, and 2) what they are taking with them. One client, leaving a particularly difficult job and workplace which had taken a serious emotional toll on her sense of self-esteem and competence, listed specific events, physical symptoms, challenging coworkers, and hard feelings on her "leaving behind" paper. On the "taking with me" sheet, she was able to enumerate new skills, colleagues she felt close to, and strengths she had developed or claimed during her tenure in her job. I find, regardless of the situation, the process of articulating both begins to create a space where healing can enter. Once the situation is seen through the lens of both crisis and potential source of positive, there is a palpable shift.

Once each sheet has been completed, I invite the clients to find a way to release the bad and embrace the good. Methods of "releasing" have included burning the paper, tearing it up and flushing it down the toilet, or crumpling up the list and doing a hook shot into the garbage can. Embracing the good is typically a less active process, but clients have shared their list with a loved one, recited it out loud in our session, or quietly folded it up to put among their important papers. Spending time to contemplate the good they will carry forward with them, such as a special memory, a community, uncovered strengths, or a new skill, can lodge the benefits more firmly in their hearts and minds.

When deciding on a ritual, reflect on your intention and integrate any symbols meaningful to you. Some of my less spiritual rituals occurred in my early twenties when girlfriends and I would mark the end of a bad relationship by tearing up the ex-boyfriend's photos and burning them in the fireplace. With the increasing use of social media, I believe "unfriending" on Facebook and deleting contacts on smartphones have taken the place of fireplaces and matches! As I have matured, I have also found creating a sacred space for the ceremony to take place and ending the ritual with a blessing brings a sense of peace I now value over my younger self's outrage and anger. In their rituals, clients have used a full moon, a body of water, a special location in nature, a gathering of friends, and spiritual spaces to find a place filled with the sacredness they seek. While the location is important, what is brought into the place also requires thought. Include those things (music, wise friends, candles, scents, symbols) that nourish your soul in this process. As you begin to consider creating a ritual to honor what has been released or lost from your life, consider these factors:

- *Step one*: Prepare to do the ritual: Does anyone else need to be involved in designing the ritual? A fellow employee and I were asked to speak at the funeral of a well-respected work colleague and close friend who had died unexpectedly. Knowing her life, friendship, and her death had touched the whole office, we set up a meeting and invited everyone who could attend. It was important to us to gain their ideas and input in order to create a eulogy reflecting the hearts of all of her colleagues, not solely ours.

- *Step two*: Set your intention—What do you want to accomplish with this ritual? How do you want to feel when it is over? Liberated? Calm? Nurtured? Connected to your heart? What form should the ritual take, given the intention and the hoped-for outcome? Are there actions particularly meaningful to you? Many people find meditation or prayer helps them to become centered in their intention and thus include them in their ritual.

- *Step three*: Include a meaningful symbol—Are there pictures, belongings, gifts, letters, books, or other things representative of the loss or change to you? Imber-Black and Roberts point out the ability for symbols to give voice to feelings, beliefs, and our connection to the Divine without a single word being uttered. They can provide a bond with the past, representing what we are leaving behind, as well as connect us to what we believe lies ahead. Some clients, when faced with the end of a relationship or marriage, have made a ceremony of passing on or giving away clothes, jewelry, art, silverware, letters, and other objects as they release a loved one or trying time in their past. One of my client's sons, for example, experienced a painfully difficult senior year at his private high school. It was with great pleasure when, rather than donating the uniforms back to the school, she and he ceremoniously dumped them into a garbage bag and threw them away. It signaled to them they had cut the last ties to the school and the painful memories formed there.

- *Step four*: Locate or create a sacred space—Where should this ritual take place? Is there a location—a room, a place in nature, or a geographical spot representing, in some way, the transition, ending, or loss you are recognizing?

Early in our marriage, Vito and I had gone to Ireland and visited the wild and barren lands of Connemara on Ireland's West Coast. Ireland connected to Vito's soul in a way he could never articulate. When Vito died, Nick and I intuitively knew we needed a ceremony, the two of us alone, to say our private goodbyes to Vito, and Ireland was the obvious choice.

- *Step five*: Find a prayer or blessing—Does a certain prayer, a poem, a story, or a quote bring you a sense of peace or provide a sense of closure to the crisis? I will suggest clients consider using the Buddhist loving kindness prayer as a way to release what has been, particularly when saying farewell to an individual—beloved or challenging. The version I like is:

May you know peace
May you know love
And may you see the light and beauty of your own true nature.

As Imber-Black and Roberts, two noted family therapists, point out, rituals give us time and space to process the transitions in our lives.[27] In whatever way you choose to mark this transition in your life, allow yourself the time to contemplate and be conscious about what has occurred during this time of challenge. By doing so, you can be mindful about the changes you are bringing forward as you go into the next stage of your life.

STRATEGY #3. BE PATIENT WITH YOUR GRIEF.

I have found grief can be both unpredictable and unexpectedly complex. While sadness is the most obvious component of a personal or professional loss, my clients regularly experience other, sometimes private, aspects to their grief. Uncovering, naming, and processing the different strata loss can contain can be a messy and time-consuming process.

William, a forty-five-year-old hospital administrator, came to see me because he was struggling with coming to terms with his wife's death several years previously. They had been a sparkling, witty, professional couple. His wife, Shelly, had been a senior partner in a prestigious law firm; he was well-known for his work in health care. When he came home from a business trip to find her dead from a suicide, his world fell apart. It continued to crumble as her well-hidden gambling debts began to surface. Shocked, feeling betrayed and foolish, he was still stuck between anger and grief despite the passage of years. As we talked, we began to sort through the layers of his despair, pausing to honor each of the emotions wrapped up in his loss. Only then could he begin to remember the woman he had loved and begin to move on to the next phase of his life without her.

While we are typically granted the space and time we need when we lose a loved one, other losses are not as easily accommodated in busy lives. And yet, it's important to find the time and space to process what has been lost during a crisis—a home, a marriage or significant relationship, a possibility, a potential future, or an aspect of ourselves, such as health or mobility, we had believed more secure than it was. Whether it be a quiet evening, a long weekend, a sabbatical, or time with (or away from) friends, reflect and articulate what has been lost, left behind, or changed in this ending.

While finding the time is crucial, we must also be gentle with the inconsistency and various forms of our grief. It can feel impossibly leaden one day, sitting heavily on our hearts, and the next day, while we are feeling a small amount of energy return, make a sharp and unexpected appearance. Grief has the ability to take us from "doing okay, thank you" to gutted in the time it takes us to listen to the first lines of a song or smell a familiar scent. For me, hearing the first lines of Elvis Presley's "I Can't Help Falling in Love with You" will still bring a fleeting appearance of grief with it. It was "our" song and always will be. For other clients, it can be a smell or sight they connect with the one whom they lost—a certain aftershave or a restaurant where they dined on special occasions. There are any number of invisible land mines of grief only identifiable once they trigger the memories. The losses accompanying a serious life crisis can take multiple iterations to understand and experience, and the path through them is rarely linear or predictable. Clients consistently come into therapy wondering why they are feeling down, tearful, or easily upset. As we sort through possibilities, frequently we uncover a connection to the anniversary of a death, loss, or significant life transition. Once uncovered, they can begin to process the relationship between their mood and the anniversary. Inevitably, an unrecognized part of their loss lies at the base of the current grief. Anne Lamott, one of my all-time favorite authors, writes in *Traveling Mercies: Some Thoughts on Faith*, "Grief, as I read somewhere once, is a lazy Susan. One day it is heavy and underwater and the next day it spins and stops at loud and rageful, and the next day at wounded keening, and the next day numbness, silence." I have been taken unaware by the sudden shift from sad to gut-sobbing and back to calm as well. Our insistence we be able to anticipate the road grief will take us on only adds to the difficult and challenging emotions we face on our journey towards a measure of peace.

Because most of my clients are middle-aged and older, our therapy sessions have been full of the life-stage endings they are going through—children going off to college, children being married, retirement, selling homes where their families were raised to downsize into a space appropriate to their current situation. It is natural, perhaps tempting, to let those chapter conclusions pass without marking them in some way. I have found, nonetheless, creating some small ritual to mark the ending of one phase and the beginning of another seems to be a way to ground them gently into the movement between the past and the new present. In sessions with parents whose children are readying to leave for their first year in college, we talk about what might represent to them that this stage of their parenting life is coming to an end. We speak of going through school papers and artwork to winnow it down to the most important or special remembrances of their college-aged children's earlier schooling, cleaning out their rooms and organizing them at last without teenage interference, or moving the video games to a less obvious spot. The actions need not be an elaborate ceremony; what counts is the intention behind them. As my clients consider what actions to take, I ask them what they want to bring into their lives in this new phase. That intention forms the base of the ritual they create.

My experience is that, by consciously bringing "what's next?" into the ending, my clients find their ways forward more easily (for some suggestions on how to figure out "what's next" see "Envision a New Life for Yourself" in Chapter 3 of this stage). It is when they come home to an empty nest after dropping their child off at school, sign the divorce papers, or wake up the first morning of retirement with a blank slate in front of them, that the enormity of the changes can be daunting. Planning to take a midweek vacation with their spouses, finally free of the logistics of teenagers at home, packing away the wedding photos of now-defunct marriages, going to spas, or planning cruises are visible signs to themselves and others they have moved into the adventure of creating new lives. Those plans serve to light the next steps on the paths in front of them so when they are ready, they can find their way more effortlessly into those spaces awaiting them—spaces of possibilities.

STRATEGY #4. LET YOUR WISDOM GUIDE YOU.

In the same manner as every crisis is as individual as a fingerprint of the people involved in it, the path through crisis is equally personal. I've learned in my years as a therapist and widow there is no simple fail-proof plan or method for grieving, despite our human desire for a trustworthy road map. Cultures throughout the world have created rituals and beliefs about the proper processing of grief. The Victorians had this down to an art: clothing (colors and fabrics), jewelry, ability to socialize, periods of time one was expected to mourn—every aspect was captured in manuals households of a certain socioeconomic status were expected to follow. In our current culture, there still are numerous myths about grief—what it should look like, how long it should last, and the appropriate behavior for the one who is grieving. The reality is everyone needs to find his or her own way through loss. Kubler-Ross, confirming the importance of this individuality in her final book *On Grief and Grieving: Finding the Meaning of Grief Through the Five Stages of Grief*, said "They (the stages) were never meant to help tuck messy emotions into neat packages. They are responses to loss many people have, but there is not a typical response to loss, as there is no typical loss. Our grieving is as individual as our lives."

In a variety of ways, the experience of grief at the end of a crisis can be similar to the shock at the beginning of it: the physical effects as well as some of the mental and emotional ones. Consequently, it may be helpful to return to "The First Stage: Surviving the Initial Shock" for some ideas or reminders on dealing with these reactions. But, most importantly, listen to your heart's voice more than anyone else's—despite the fact it may seem odd. Rationality can rarely (if ever) completely explain the loss of someone or something extraordinarily important to you and so it makes sense, at least to me, that rational behavior may not be the exclusive way through the grieving process. Or, as Thomas Moore in *Dark Nights of the Soul: Finding Your Way Through Life's Ordeals* points out, "You may have to do some crazy things, because, when the soul is touched at its very foundations, only a departure from the rational can restore it." (p. 258) One of my clients used the settlement she received after the sudden and shocking death of her husband to get a facelift. She felt as if the mess he had left her to clean up had taken years off her life and this was a way to regain some of the lost time. It made sense to her—and that is what counted.

Some ways to figure out what may be most helpful to you:

- If you have a whim, give in to it unless it's illegal or harmful to yourself or others. Recently I heard an example of someone who found an unusual way to cope with her grief and loss when her husband died unexpectedly. A lovely, conservative woman in her seventies chose to get her nose pierced, get a tattoo, and spend a summer motorcycling through Europe. Her actions reminded her she was tough enough to face whatever challenges might come her way.

- If you are unsure if an activity is right for you, create a visualization of yourself actually engaged in the activity. For example, if you want to skydive, imagine yourself high in the air, parachute strapped on your back, looking out of the airplane door ready to jump. Does it feel good to you to envision yourself doing it? Or do you find yourself feeling uncomfortably anxious or tense when considering it? Listening to your body's reactions to each possibility is a good way to find out if it will be helpful to you while you grieve.

- My sister-in-law, a stay-at-home mom who had been actively and beautifully involved in her children's lives, took a proactive step in creating her new life as an empty nester. During the senior year of her last child at home, she set up an art studio in their garage and gathered a small group of artists who wanted to work together, share, and encourage one another in their painting and art exhibitions. Now, a decade later, the studio still nurtures her art group as well as provides her with space uniquely her own within their large home.

- Stephanie, another client who was dealing with an unwanted and unexpected divorce, was struggling with finding a way out of her anger and frustration. She was used to putting family first, so I urged her to take one self-nurturing step towards her new life. After some initial resistance, she made a reservation at a well-known spa on the east coast during its off-season. Originally worried about being off on her own, she discovered both the delight of unstructured time and the encouragement of the other women at the spa. They shared their stories of grief and survival with her, letting her recognize similar possibilities for herself. She returned home more grounded and secure in the belief she could make it through this difficult and challenging time.

- Through the process of letting go, grieving, listening to our hearts, and trusting ourselves to discern the pace and path of our process, the emergence from the cocoon is initiated. Yet it is crucial to remember endings are also their own form of beginnings. Whether they are anticipated or unexpected, slow to arrive or occurring without warning, they signal a transition in our lives. When the endings are a welcome punctuation point, we are served best by moving thoughtfully and purposefully from where we were to where we are going. We have undoubtedly exhausted ourselves during the challenging times. There is wisdom in making sure our balance is steady, our gas tanks have been refilled, and our footprints are well-planted before beginning again.

CHAPTER 2:
REPLENISH YOUR RESOURCES

It is our best work that God wants, not the dregs of our exhaustion. I think he must prefer quality to quantity.
–George MacDonald

The "hit" the body takes during a crisis cannot be underestimated or denied. My client Jim, a senior executive with a large biochemical company, after going through both a traumatic divorce and a life-threatening illness within the space of five years, was struck by adrenal fatigue, a syndrome generally associated with prolonged stress where the adrenal glands operate at a sub-optimal level. While most people experience less dramatic symptoms than Jim, more than one friend or client has complained to me about their slow progress back to "their old selves." When Nick was born, a good friend gave me some powerfully wise advice, which I remembered but didn't follow. She said, "Six weeks after you give birth, you will assume you are back to normal. Six months later, you'll realize how crazy that belief was." She was right. Because we are sadly unaware of how badly our resources can be depleted while we are managing crises, we can find ourselves on a much longer path to recovery than we had imagined. Once the crisis has ended, moving toward your post-crisis life requires close attention to what you need to do to rebuild your strength to get there.

STRATEGIES

STRATEGY #1. SURRENDER THE TIMING OF RECOVERY.

Judith Orloff, in *The Ecstasy of Surrender: 12 Surprising Ways Letting Go Can Empower Your Life*, defines surrender as "the grace of letting go at the right moment—the ability to accept what is, to exhale, and to flow downstream with the cycles of life instead of battling them, obsessively attaching to people and outcomes, and anxiously brooding." My clients—goal-oriented, hard-charging, and successful—find this as challenging to do as I. It can seem especially impossible once the hyper-focus of a crisis has ended. As we finally pause to take a deep breath, there can be a huge *"Now what?"* This is usually when the critical voices reemerge—chanting their litany of shame over tasks left undone. It is extremely easy to jump into feverish activity, addressing all the tasks, chores, and responsibilities left undone by necessity or exhaustion when our crises took center stage. Undoubtedly, it can feel good to get those tasks accomplished and off the list, yet it is rarely what would be most helpful for us, despite the obvious short-term rewards. It is also extremely counterproductive to the goal of getting past exhaustion! Instead, set aside some time in a quiet spot and go back to the answers you came up with when evaluating your "big rock" priorities.

Then, as you move forward into what *has* to be done (bills to be paid, a career to manage, children and family to care for), be sure to find some space for taking action on the areas identified above. Most of my clients find what needs the most attention, post-crisis, is replenishing their physical, mental, emotional, and spiritual resources.

STRATEGY #2. RETRIEVE WHAT HAS BEEN PUT ASIDE.

It is important to recognize the parts of your life you've put on hold or overused in order to get through times of crisis—times when it's easy for us to lose track of our authentic selves. It wasn't until Vito died and I had time to reflect and journal about what I was feeling, experiencing, and wanting that I began to understand how much of the essential me I had ignored or shoved down due to the demands of my career and my family life, even before the illnesses of my men. Dr. Kenneth C. Ruge, author of *Where Do I Go From Here? An Inspirational Guide to Making Authentic Career and Life Choices*, uses the term "true self"—which is, among other ineffable qualities, the part of us uniquely ours which holds the knowledge of why we are here. Ruge suggests finding it requires the patience to follow a mostly circuitous and meandering path and uses the example of Russian nesting dolls as a metaphor for the process. Each time one doll is revealed, there is still another to explore; in the same manner, finding our true selves requires much unveiling. He also talks about the importance of how you shape the process of finding those parts of you that may have wandered off while you weren't paying attention. Ruge offers five different aspects to consider, including where and how you physically want to be, how you spend your time, whom you wish to connect with regularly, and the sensory input you want to allow or invite into your life. As you seek to reawaken those facets of you which you lost during or before a crisis, consider these elements.

Roberta initially came to therapy because of a sense of dullness and discontent with her life. Several years earlier she had been arbitrarily fired from a prestigious position and her self-esteem had taken a huge hit. In the process of regaining traction in her career and meeting some exceptionally ambitious goals for herself, she had been hyper-focused on work and family. With her most recent promotion to a senior VP position within her healthcare firm, those fears had begun to subside, but as they did, her unhappiness with her life began to surface. As we explored her values and talked about what excited her, a desire for spiritual scholarship and connection to her heritage arose. She was an active member in her church but she wanted a deeper understanding than her current religious study was able to provide. As we brainstormed ways for her to pursue her passion, the increase in her energy level was obvious. Roberta's pursuit of what fed her spirit has led her to the Holy Land multiple times and spurred her to take on more leadership within her religious community.

In the process of keeping step with the logistics and needs associated with the crisis you have recently been through, your spirit may have lost its ability to attune inward. Taking the time to stop and listen to yourself, and exploring your needs and desires as you move forward, can bring a sense of confidence and direction to the steps you take, once you are ready.

CHAPTER 3:
TAKE FLIGHT

You were born with wings.
You are not meant for crawling, so don't.
You have wings.
Learn to use them and fly.
–Rumi

With Vito's passing and Nick's return to college, I suddenly had un-fettered leeway to design my life. Yet, I found myself filling the time autonomy provided in tactical and unintentional ways—task lists multiplied, my online solitaire game improved significantly, and I was scheduling dinners with friends at an almost frenetic pace. I also found it easy to fall back into my role of caretaker, spending time with friends who were struggling with their own challenges.

I woke up one day and realized I was blowing my opportunity to create the life I wanted. There was white space in my life and if I weren't careful, it would fill up with minutiae and other people's priorities. I saw, in a moment of clarity, I had become so over-identified with the role of caretaker it had become a default mode for me. As long as I stayed in my familiar role, I was safe and needed, but I wasn't living my life—I was ignoring my dreams and goals. I knew I had to do something to shake myself out of the rut I had fallen into. Within an hour, I had used frequent flier miles to book a flight to Paris, my favorite city and a place where life's possi-bilities have repeatedly appeared clearer to me.

Post-crisis, we may not have a clear vision of where we are go-ing—so much of our internal landscape has changed. Finding our way forward can be a trial-and-error process—it takes time and involves some missteps, adventures, and calculated risks. We have changed and perhaps, so has the path we will take forward. By studying the maps of possibilities, trusting our own innate wisdom about what makes sense to us now and the signs we may receive, we can begin to find our way.

THE FIFTH STAGE

STRATEGIES

STRATEGY #1. REDEFINE YOUR WORLD.

Spurred by the challenge of a dear friend to make the house my own shortly after Vito's death, I struggled to identify what pleased me and fit the life I was creating. For twenty-five years, I had been part of a partnership where decisions were made encompassing both of our wishes and viewpoints. It was a skill critical to a successful marriage but was no longer relevant to my life. Initially the process was fraught with stress and frustration but slowly, and eventually, joyfully, the vision about the house and my life became clearer, and a house once decorated with the colors and materials of the earth now reflects the light-loving mermaid who lives in my soul.

As you begin to explore the ways in which you may or may not have changed, consider:

- When you walk into your home or office, what draws your attention? Is it pleasing or nurturing to you? Does it feel jarring or outdated in some way?

- Have you found your taste in music, clothing, or food changed? Clients can find the comfort food they had relied on during the crisis gets shifted to more normal, healthy eating once the crisis has abated.

- Do you find yourself wanting to engage in different conversations or perhaps fewer conversations than before? A friend and I recently discussed how our interest and participation in gossip had decreased after our own life crises. Somehow seeing a parent (her mother) or husband (Vito) through death

167

seemed to render unpalatable the quibbling and complaining happening in a workplace or with friends.

- How do you see yourself differently now? How does the change in you play out at work or with friends? Do they experience you the same way? For some clients, defining themselves as a survivor gives them a sense of pride and self-esteem. Others avoid the term, believing it anchors them to an unpleasant past.

STRATEGY #2. VISUALIZE A NEW FUTURE.

Similar to when you were regaining your balance from the shock the crisis produced in your life, it is extremely helpful to have a focal point on the horizon when emerging. By developing a vision of how you want your life to be and what you want to be doing, even if it is only a rough draft, you begin to move towards it. Anyone who has read about the Law of Attraction or watched the movie *What the Bleep Do We Know?* has been introduced to the idea that we bring into our lives what we can imagine. Consequently, finding ways to create a visual representation of what we are choosing to pursue or create allows us to more effectively focus on it. Some ideas might be to:

- Create a vision board—A vision board is a visual representation, through images, quotes, phrases, words, or affirmations, which captures the essence of your goal. They have been used in therapy and metaphysical practices for a variety of reasons. While this was traditionally done using books or magazines, one of the top self-help trends at the time of this writing is creating a vision board via Pinterest (a web and application-based tool allowing users to search, collect, share, and store visual images).

A close friend of mine found the job of her dreams after a layoff but it came with a price. Her new boss required his employees to live fairly close to the office, which was several miles away from where she currently lived. A long-time believer of the power of visualization, she began to cut out words and images from magazines, creating a vision board of the place where she wanted herself and her young daughter to live. She wrote things like "community" and "friends," glued pictures of a pool, an open floor plan, and trees. Several months into her house search, she walked into what is now her home. It has a pool, an open floor space, beautiful old trees, and a group of families who welcomed her warmly. Her daughter already has a new best friend in the neighborhood, and equally exciting for me, she lives about five minutes away from my home!

The possibilities are endless when using a vision board. Its power lies in the ability to first visualize what you want in your life through pictures and words, making it easier to recognize when you face choices which might bring you towards your goals or take you further away from them. A vision board is intensely personal and for those with whom the idea resonates, an excellent companion on the journey towards their desired outcomes.

- Pay attention to your dreams—Some psychologists, me included, believe dreams can be 1) random images and thoughts—flotsam and jetsam of the day making its way through our psyche, 2) a way of psychologically processing issues troubling to us or that we are working through, or 3) a form of Divine or inner guidance. In a form typically more symbolic than concrete or linear, our dreams can give us messages, clues, or other kinds of insight into the workings of our psyche. Mona Lisa Shultz, author of *Awakening Intuition: Using Your Mind-Body Network for Insight and Healing* and a medical doctor with a Ph.D. in neuroscience, describes our dreams as one of the ways in which our brains attempt to solve problems, or examine the choices we have in our lives. With our critical, typically fault-finding frontal

lobes safely asleep, our possibilities open up for us to consider, try out, or, in our dream experience, live out.

My clients and friends will bring dreams to me so we can explore
together what they might be telling us. Consistently I find the
dreams are partnering with us as we explore parts of their lives. One
of my clients who has been through several years of personal and
professional crises is starting to perceive the impact stifling her emotions has had on her psyche. Initially unwilling to talk about anything other than practical logistics, she has gradually allowed herself
to experience some emotions. Her dreams in the last year have been
full of water (a common dream symbol for emotion)—huge bodies
or rivers of it, allowing her in a safe way to experience some of what
she has been keeping at bay. As she becomes more acquainted with
the emotional part of her she denied for most of her life, she is also
beginning to appreciate the highly competent, wise woman she has
always been. Her story reminded me that, as we begin to explore
the messages our souls are trying to tell us in our dreams, patterns
start to emerge, bringing with them both insight and wisdom.
Dreams can point the way to the hidden, squelched, and unloved
parts of ourselves. There is much to be learned by paying attention
to the messages our dreams are sending. Try tapping into your internal guidance system by:

- *Step one*: Buying and using a dream journal. Judith Orloff's
  book, *Second Sight,* suggests keeping a journal to record
  your dreams is a way of "giving yourself permission to
  dream."

- *Step two*: Before you go to bed at night, write a question in
  your dream journal. Where do you want more guidance in
  your life? Your work? Your relationships? Your health?

- *Step three*: If it feels right to you, ask for Divine assistance in
  resolving the problem or answering the question.

- *Step four*: Tell yourself you will remember your dreams in the morning.

- *Step five*: When you awaken, before doing anything else (in particular before you turn on any electronic devices), write down any fragments of dreams you remember.

Repeat the process over the course of a week or until you have received a clear answer. If you haven't received clarity about your question, go back through your journal at the end of the week and highlight repeating phrases, themes, words, or images. Pay attention to if there is a message in them.

STRATEGY #3. STEP FORWARD WITH A PLAN.

Visions and ideas about the life you want to live are an excellent first step, but they require practical actions to bring to fruition. As I used to teach in change management workshops, inspiration and motivation without action merely leads to some interesting but aimless wandering about!

Using your vision board or any other method you've used to decide what you want to bring into your life, write down specific action steps you will need to take to move you in that direction. Don't worry about sequencing them at the beginning; get them down. Once you have your list, pick one thing you can do right now to begin the process towards achieving your goal. Finish it and then pick another, and another, and another. Don't overcommit yourself; just get started. If you need some ideas to jump-start your process, try these:

- Take twenty—Diane Conway wrote an inspiring book, *What Would You Do if You Had No Fear? Living Your Dreams While Quakin' In Your Boots*, which I read when I was feeling stuck in my life and in serious need of motivation. On impulse, I reached out and set up some coaching sessions with her. I knew I needed a community of support as I took my next steps but I also knew I needed someone to keep me accountable. Diane had a variety of solid suggestions but, as good coaches do, she also helped remind me of what I already knew. Of the plentiful and useful suggestions she made, I found the Twenty-Minute Miracle most helpful. Briefly, it involves setting a timer for twenty minutes to make progress on your goals (for more details and a step-by-step explanation, check out Diane's book!).

• Explore your interests—Mimi came to therapy partially because her graphic arts business was experiencing a downturn. She had had her business for thirty years and was feeling restless in her career. It was premature financially to retire but she needed something else to fill her life. As we talked, one of the areas of her life where she showed the most interest and energy was her love of indigenous art, particularly from South America. For the next couple of weeks, she tried several different ideas: taking a class at the nearby university in indigenous art, studying it on her own, making a tour of galleries showing the art of indigenous peoples, and joining a group engaged in helping indigenous artists sell their work in the U.S. In our session after her first meeting with the group, I saw enthusiasm and energy I hadn't seen before. She had found some of her "tribe" and was excited about what might come next in this adventure she had begun.

• Take some practice runs—If you're not absolutely sure how you want to change, try following a path for a while. For example, if you're interested in working at a non-profit, have lunch with its executive director or volunteer to do some fundraising for them. They will be delighted to have you. If you believe you may want to move to the beach, research possible locations and rent a condo or home for a week or two, immersing yourself in the day-to-day of your chosen town. In this digital age, it's possible to pursue most interests without leaving, at least initially, your own home. Eventually, you will find something compelling enough to make the way forward obvious.

STRATEGY #4. TAKE YOUR TIME.

One of the most creative and touching gifts we were given following Vito's death was a plant holding a live cocoon. A week later, the cocoon began to act as if something was about to happen and so we sat, my parents, our neighbors, and I, waiting for this miracle of transformation to take place. An eternity later (perhaps only an hour), a butterfly dragged itself to the top of the cocoon and shivered in the sixty-degree weather. Its wings opened cautiously, flapping and stilling, working up the strength it needed to take its first winged leap of faith and instinct. As we held our breaths, the butterfly launched itself towards the brightly covered lantana shrub near it and flopped into the orange, yellow, and scarlet blossoms. We watched as it drank in the sustenance it needed for what seemed to be another hour. As we watched it examine carefully its new environment, trying out the tools it had developed during the dark stage of its cocooning, and find its way anew, I realized the gift I was being given. I was being shown the way by a small insect who had only its innate wisdom to lead it. Go slowly, it seemed to be saying; take your time, look around, make sure you are ready. Ahead might be the greatest gift our time of crisis can offer—transformation and wings.

THE SIXTH STAGE: PAN FOR THE GOLD

Learn the alchemy true human beings know.
The moment you accept what troubles you've been
given, the door will open.
–Rumi

Crises are crucibles in our lives. We are altered forever by the disruption in our lives. In the singular, survival-minded focus crisis can demand of us, the dross of the mundane melts from our day-to-day lives. Both our strengths and our vulnerabilities, highlighted against the backdrop of our tough times, become clear to us and others. In turn, the ways in which we perceive ourselves and our lives may also change. We have seen new strengths emerge, fought back fears, shattered old beliefs. We view life and the people around us differently. They have not necessarily changed, but we have. But the question is, *how* have we changed? Has the crucible heated us to the point where we are irreparably damaged, or has the crisis yielded some nuggets of pure gold?

There is an alchemical process that can occur in a crisis. Research is still uncovering the antecedents, personality traits, and other factors which seemingly make some individuals more or less prone to emerge from serious crises with Frankl's "tragic optimism" or the current term, "post-traumatic growth." We do recognize it is not a universal outcome, but neither is it an unusual one. In 2004, Alex Linley and Stephen Joseph, researchers on the topic of post-traumatic growth and the authors of *Trauma, Growth, and Recov-*

ery: Positive Psychological Perspectives on Post-Traumatic Stress, reviewed approximately forty studies to determine the percentage of individuals who reported some kind of positive change following a traumatic event and found the numbers ranged from thirty to seventy percent. We have found, however, there are some personalities and characteristics which apparently lend themselves more readily to growing from a crisis. Lawrence Calhoun and Richard Tedeschi report in their book, *Facilitating Post-Traumatic Growth: A Clinician's Guide,* individuals "who have a more complex cognitive style, who have higher levels of optimism and hope, who are more extroverted, who are creative thinkers, and who are open to the possibility of new experiences may be somewhat more likely to experience post-traumatic growth." (p. 15)

So, what are the ways, if we are so inclined, to facilitate our own growth after a crisis? For us to find the gold or the growth in the challenges we have gone through, I believe we must first find a way to sort through what happened—not only chronologically, but also physically, emotionally, and spiritually. For me the sorting process occurred through a considerable number of extended conversations with trusted friends, through writing this story multiple times, and simply through the passage of time. When I paused to examine my journey through the eyes of my friends or from a perspective more objective or further removed, new wisdom emerged and different scars became visible. For example, eight years (at this writing) after Vito's death, I can recognize my contributions to the failures in our marriage as well as its successes, but also I doubt I will ever hear Nick voice a bodily complaint without having a first, initial reaction of "Is it cancer?"

Once we have begun to understand what has happened, we can begin to discern what has changed in us—the positive and adverse outcomes of our journey through crisis—and how those changes impact our perspective on life. With this knowledge firmly in our grasp, we can then set our course. What will we now choose to do and how will we spend our lives, now we fully comprehend how precious and challenging and rewarding it can be?

CHAPTER 1:
LOOK FOR GOLD AMIDST
THE DEBRIS

Where there is ruin, there is hope for a treasure.
–Rumi

Early in my career as a consulting psychologist, I was trained in the art of providing leadership and performance feedback to corporate personnel. My job was to help them sort through both positive and constructive feedback from ten or fifteen co-workers in order to create a development plan for their future professional growth. Because the amount of information they received could seem overwhelming, I quickly understood my job was to help them find the two or three nuggets of information most useful to them in their roles and their careers. But in order to help them make sense of the information and find a way to make it beneficial to them, I first had to understand the person I was coaching.

For the first twenty or thirty minutes of our two-hour session, I would enquire about their personal and professional goals and the values they wanted to be known for, as well as what they viewed as success—in their professional roles and in their personal lives. We also talked about how they saw their strengths and weaknesses, and how they believed others perceived them. Once I had a context, we would review the feedback, looking for recurring themes and important information. It could be painful for them, seeing in the data where their behavior was not viewed as positively as they had hoped. In those liminal moments—between hearing the feedback

179

and finding a way to bring it into their lives—I would liken their process to a gold miner's, as he or she had to dig through a pan of sludge, rock, and water to find nuggets. Saving the entire contents of the pan, meant bringing home a load of useless debris, but equally true, if the pan's whole contents were discarded, there was a risk of missing something—possibly of great value. Our job, I told them, was to find the nuggets and claim them for their value while leaving behind the dregs.

I believe we have the same choice, post-crisis. We can toss it, the experience, completely out—do our best to forget the crisis ever happened or take it all home with us and let it be an ongoing story of personal devastation. There are indeed significant ways in which a crisis can and frequently does change our lives and our perspectives adversely. Another choice is to swirl the contents around and look through it to determine if there might possibly be something else there, beyond the potentially negative post-crisis outcomes in your life. I have worked with clients in my therapy practice who have dealt with their crises in each of these ways. By contemplating the possibility of something more than other loss, pain, and frustration, clients frequently discover some nuggets of gold—emergent or well-forged strengths, expanded perspectives, hard-won wisdom, spiritual growth, gratitude, compassion, appreciation, or newfound purpose.

STRATEGIES

STRATEGY #1. WRITE YOUR OWN NARRATIVE.

As a therapist, I have long understood the power of a story. How my clients talk about their lives, the ways in which they explain what is happening to them or has happened to them, define, I believe, their experiences. I listen carefully as they describe the important events in their lives—the words they choose to tell their stories are the breadcrumbs showing me how to follow them into their deepest thoughts and beliefs.

As humans, we have told stories for millennia—it is our way of sharing wisdom, of teaching, of understanding what has happened and what might. Immediately after a crisis has abated and you have recovered sufficiently to begin to wonder about who you are now and how you've changed, one of the best ways to make sense of what has happened to you is to tell your story—to others or simply to yourself. You have perhaps already started this process if you spent a significant amount of time fretting about the crisis while it was going on. Calhoun and Tedeschi have found that rumination, the process by which you turn the events of the crisis (or other problems) over and over in your mind, may actually be a necessary prerequisite for post-traumatic growth.[28] Through our pondering, as we are trying to understand what has happened or figure out solutions in order to regain our senses of equilibrium, we can set the foundation for future growth.

In his bestselling book, *Dark Nights of the Soul: A Guide to Finding Your Way Through Life's Ordeals*, Thomas Moore shares his belief that talking about the journey we have been on is an important way of making sense of what has happened to us. He sees it as not only a form of catharsis but also as the pathway towards transformation. Moore, a trained psychotherapist, offers sound advice about how to tell your story, including the importance of finding someone who will listen with respect. If you can find someone who will ask you the kinds of questions you need to begin to put the experiences into the context of your life, so much the better. His point is not everyone has the right or the skills to hear your story. Most of us have experienced the frustration of trying to share something important with someone whose own needs, frustrations, or fears prevent them from truly being present to our words and our emotions. I was repeatedly surprised by how people projected onto me their own fears or beliefs about what it would feel like to lose a partner or spouse. And frequently, in the face of their story, I would shut down rather than fight for the space to tell my own. It is critical when deciding whom to share your story with, particularly as you are beginning to make sense of it yourself, you find a kind, receptive ear—someone who dearly much wants to comprehend the details of your experience and what it has meant to you.

Like Moore, I have found my clients tell their stories in numerous different ways: letters, stories, paintings, poems, treasured objects, photographs, and, for some, songs. As they bring those mementos to our sessions, the stories of what and who they have lost begin to come out. One client, early in my therapeutic practice, would bring the paintings she had done during the time between our sessions. Slowly, as we contemplated at the form, the subject, the colors, and the emotions of her paintings, her story of abuse and grief intertwined began to emerge. As her childhood traumas came more fully into the light, we were able to examine them together. We were able to unearth how they had shaped her life—for good and for not-so-good. And, as we examined at the ways the paintings spoke for her pain, her suffering, and her anger, she was able to recognize the destructive nature of the path she had been on—prostitution and drugs—and begin to make different decisions for her life. As she built a new life on the strengths she had developed in order to withstand the abuse, she found the beginnings of compassion for her choices, for herself, and ultimately for her abuser. With compassion and courage on her side, her protective grip on the grievous hurts and decisions of her past began to loosen, allowing her to open up to a different, more promising future.

As you write your story, recognize this may only be the first time. Each time you revisit it, if you do, you may find more truths, more gifts, and perhaps more grief and sadness. But if your experience is like mine, the return will be worth it.

- *Step one*: Find a way to begin—To start the process of telling your story, use a timeline, or simple narrative, and write down what happened during this crisis. Find a quiet place and time, say a prayer (if the idea resonates for you), light a candle, put on music, dress in your comfiest clothes. Set the stage for the sacred journey into your crisis. If it helps, ask a close friend or family member to answer some of the questions listed in Appendix A. It might work best if you take a question at a time and journal your answer, dictate your thoughts into a voice transcription application, or tell a friend who will take notes. This is an epic tale and should be given some reverence and time to complete.

- *Step two*: Synthesize—As you read back over the answers to the questions listed in Appendix A, what positive and negative themes emerge? Did you find strength within yourself you had never recognized or appreciated before? Have you lost a sense of security? Were you humbled by the friends who stepped forward? Did some friends disappoint you? Did your faith play a huge role in getting you through the hard parts, or has it taken a hit? Is it simply that you made it through a time you thought you couldn't survive? If it appeals to you, give your story a title and identify the key players in it.

My client Bridget had already experienced the multiple gut-punches of the deaths of her sister, her best friend, and her nephew within an obscenely short period of time when she came home to find her husband bloody and dead on the floor. The autopsy revealed his heart attack had been caused by cocaine use—an ugly, shocking end to a marriage that had seemed, to her and everyone around her, golden. As a public figure in Dallas, she felt she had no choice but to keep secret the true cause of his death. Talking to me allowed her to share her secret and have a compassionate witness to her journey. Writing gave her the thread she needed to find her way back through the labyrinth of self-doubt, anger, and unforgiveness into which death had led her. From her process, started while she was still howling with rage and curse words, Bridget found this gold:

> *Being mad kept me connected to him, both the good and the bad…I did not want to give up that part of me that died with him. I had to give up my goddamn self-righteousness and feeling I had been wronged. I had to stop the scorecard and break out of my comfort zone of anger and resentment. Accepting that was thorny, because it meant I had to let him go. More importantly, I had to swallow the Kool-Aid of "you have to forgive yourself before you forgive others" openly.*

> *For me, there was no other choice. There wasn't a formula or great insights into God or faith or inner peace or growth. It was putting one foot in front of the other and accepting the messy imperfections of me. Accepting his death was my learner's permit to accept life's imperfections, and the big fat billboard of my own. At times, they still piss me off. The difference now is they don't fester.*

For Bridget, looking back at her journey allowed her to admit that fury served to keep her husband present in some way in her life. Yet this knowledge also gave her the choice of staying mired in resentment and betrayal or taking a path away from her wounds—allowing her to release the anger but more importantly, to find self-acceptance and self-compassion.

If writing isn't your medium, look at the questions in Appendix A and try some of the following to represent your story:

Find a book or movie capturing the essence of what you endured. If it is a book, look for images on the web or in magazines to represent your story. If a movie speaks to your experience, determine if you can locate a picture of the scene capturing what you are trying to convey, or perhaps a copy of the movie poster. Are there particularly meaningful or apt quotes from the movie or book? In *The Fault in Our Stars* Hazel—a young woman who is diagnosed with cancer—has to go to the hospital for something that turns out to be minor. Hearing the news, her mom, Frannie, says to her child, "This is just a thing, Hazel. It's a thing we can live with." That one phrase speaks to the irrevocable twist a serious illness creates in your life. Everything gets reduced to the question, "Can we live with this?" Nothing else ever has the same importance again.

Return to the films, books, and/or images expressing, for you, the ways in which you've changed. Reading Elizabeth Lesser's book, *Broken Open: How Difficult Times Help Us Grow*, during the time I was making sense of my journey resonated deeply with me, as did this quote: "Whatever is happening, whatever is changing, whatever is going or not going according to my plans—I release my hold on it. I leave behind who I perceive myself to be, who I want to be, what I want the world to be. I come home to the great peace of the present moment." (p. 268) It spoke to who I had tried to be during my three years of crisis, although I failed as often as I succeeded in my intention.

The Smith Center for Healing and the Arts is a gallery in Washington, DC exhibiting art that "explores the innate connection between healing and creativity." With this in mind, create a piece of art to symbolize your journey. Sculpture, painting, mosaic, stained glass and other forms of creativity can lend themselves to your expressiveness, as can dance or music.

As you pull your story from your experiences and memories of the crisis, look for clues about how your path through the crisis has changed you. In what ways has your perspective on life shifted to the negative? Where have you lost or found hope or optimism? Where have you discovered positive changes? The answer, if you are like me and my clients, will continue to evolve and change as future life experiences make our new perspectives, strengths, and wisdom, as well as our losses and wounds, more visible. The purpose here is not to uncover a final answer, but rather to begin to ponder a question.

STRATEGY #2. LOOK FOR NUGGETS OF GOLD.

Moving on from a crisis and seeing growth can be difficult, indeed daunting. Sometimes, especially in the wake of great loss, I find my clients unable to recognize they have changed, or moved on from the loved one who has died. A turning point with Bridget, the client mentioned earlier, came when I asked her if her growth would feel like a betrayal to her marriage. When she nodded, overcome with tears, I simply asked her, "How could you *not* have changed?" It seemed impossible to me for her to have experienced the circumstances of his death—with the deep sense of loss it brought—and remain the same. In our next session, and several times afterwards, she told me how my one question had shifted her from the stuck place she had been in, allowing her to begin to claim her new self and therefore start the process of living the life in front of her. My point was that crisis, death, traumatic experiences—every one of those events will change the person who goes through it. The question is not whether we have changed but *how* we have changed—both for the positive and for the negative. Crises and our journeys through them are difficult and complex. To look for nuggets of gold and ignore the ways in which our crises may have scarred us would be to fathom only part of the experience. We can hold the pain and loss of our story, as well as the growth and blessings, in the same hand. Life, after all, contains both—and so can we.

As you review the story you wrote about your crisis and the themes emerging from it, look at your experience through the lens of the possibilities mentioned below. As you read the story, consider if any of them resonate with you and your experience. If they do, make notes for later. If not, ask yourself how else your experience might have changed you—for the better, and for the worse.

FIVE "SHAKE OUTS" OF POST-TRAUMATIC GROWTH.

Research has identified five key areas where people have discovered "gold" from the debris of their trauma or crisis. As you use the exercises above to sift through experience, pay attention to which of these, if any, are true for you:

- *Enhanced appreciation of self*. A crisis frequently creates a huge sense of vulnerability in our lives. "It couldn't happen to me" beliefs are, in one quick slash, replaced with this bald fact—bad things can indeed occur in life, despite personal precautions, prayers, and adherence to safety protocols. The world, for some, becomes a precarious place. When I asked Nick, early on, how going through cancer had impacted his life, the first thing he told me was, "I'm not invincible; in fact, no one really is. I just made the realization on a whole new level."

Yet, out of the ashes of our previous sense of safety, something more reliable can arise—a sense of one's abilities to handle, or at least survive, devastation. It can be an unwelcome gift, at least at first. Most of us would rather not grasp the extent to which we can be tested and survive—unless, of course, we don't have to experience the crucible first. It is only in retrospect, with a new crisis or challenge demanding our strengths and wisdom, we recognize the gift we have carried forward within us.

As my clients and I sort through the residue of their crisis experiences, traumas, and pain, I'm frequently the one who notices the bravery, persistence, intuition, or unwavering love they have demonstrated during the difficult times. As I dust it off and hold it up for them to see, they begin to relate other ways in which that quality has been present in their lives. And then, once seen, it becomes a greater part of how they view themselves.

A client called me the other day when he was facing a potential professional crisis which had him lying awake at night in anxiety. Robert had successfully gone through prostate cancer a few years earlier, as well as some other severe downturns in his professional life. During his treatment for cancer, we had spent a considerable amount of time exploring his fears, as well as his unaccustomed sense of vulnerability and loss of control. As we talked about the current crisis, he startled me by blurting out, "everything—the job loss, cancer, the crises I've faced moving from my old company to this one—they all have prepared me for this." As I listened, he explained he had suddenly recognized he could navigate through the uncertainty and potential consequences despite his fear that the crisis could have a negative effect on his career. His previous tough times had taught him he had the skills, strength, and resilience to handle whatever happened.

This insight echoes the Val and Linley's findings that "survivors change their self-perception in some way. They may report increased personal strength and self-reliance and experience more acceptance of their vulnerabilities and limitations, typified by a heightened awareness of their own mortality and the preciousness and fragility of life."[29] By dealing with the challenges their crises bring, survivors gain an appreciation for their ability to cope and the characteristics within themselves making such resilience possible. Or, as Nietzsche once said, "What doesn't kill me makes me stronger."

It is both perspective, which I will talk about later, and self-knowledge, which let us claim our strengths and wisdom, post-crisis. We have faced something scary and challenging, but our fear of the dark will never have the same power over us. But more importantly, we now own the knowledge of how we got through it. Alone, or with the support and guidance of others, we walked the path. We can find our way again and this becomes the foundation of our greater self-appreciation.

- *Enhanced personal relationships.* Crises can put our relationships not only with ourselves but with others under a laser-like spotlight. Priorities shift, with logistics habitually eating up any available time for intimacy. Stress piles up and people can disappoint us by their failure to show up or be who we need them to be. Yet, at the same time, there exists the potential for a strengthening of relationships when we are blessed with communities of support and a willingness to change the ways we relate to those around us.

One of the things contributing strongly to the increased intimacy or closeness individuals can feel after a crisis is more willingness to let down their defenses. For some this choice comes from being stripped down to their cores due to illness. One friend, truly looking in the mirror for the first time since chemo had taken her hair, told me it was in that moment, she realized the common humanity we shared. Recognizing the essence binding humans together made the barriers she had erected in her life seem unnecessary. For others the freedom to self-disclose comes from the loving support they have received from family, friends, and perhaps strangers during their crisis. A client going through a traumatic divorce reported how women who were strangers offered wise counsel, prayers, and other moments of grace when they found out about her struggles.

My clients and others also report their relationships undergo some changes because they feel more prepared to face hard issues and speak their truth. Dealing with severe depressions, serious illnesses, unexpected divorces, and death puts normal, challenging issues into perspective. Somehow, having dealt with difficult truths during their crises, they find it easier to confront problematic situations squarely. One client, a young investment director in her early thirties who had spent some time in an inpatient psychiatric unit for severe depression, found she was no longer willing to put up with the sarcastic put-downs and isolation her chief partner had subjected her to prior to her admission. In a calm, professional, but firm manner she called him on his behavior and the unpleasant work environment it created for her and others. To her shock, he apologized and his negative comments almost completely ceased.

Take a minute to ponder your relationships and how they may have changed since before the crisis. What has been the impact on your close relationships? What about your more casual ones? How are you different now? How do you view others differently?

- *Enhanced appreciation of life, compassion, and empathy.* One of the most common and well-known artifacts of having gone through a life-threatening illness or crisis is an awakening to the beauty and miracle of life. The movies and bookstores are full of stories, fictional and non-fictional, of individuals who find, in their recovery or final stages of their lives, life has become more valuable than ever. For some this is a lasting phenomenon and for others, it is merely transitory. Robert, shortly after finishing treatment for prostate cancer, marveled in the sense of gratitude and appreciation he felt at having been declared cancer-free. A year later, he shared with me he no longer found himself feeling the same level of appreciation for his healthy life. It had become, again, something he took for granted. Others, like my friend who recognized, in her chemo-created baldness, her connection to all humanity, have never lost the profound wonder at our divine relationship with one another.

There is also, as some of my clients have reported, a sense of community created as a result of having gone through a serious life crisis. This community is similar to the "foxhole buddies" created during World War II when two soldiers provided cover for one another in foxholes—shelters against enemy fire. People who have experienced traumatic experiences such as the death of a child, destruction of their home, a devastating divorce, violence, or a serious illness can find an increased level of compassion or empathy for others going through the same ordeal. As a result, they find themselves reaching out to help or comfort strangers in ways they previously might not have.

As I speak with clients and friends who have gone through their own challenging times, my ear is consistently tuned to the question of how they have been changed and what the crisis has taught them. What do they see now that can never be unseen?

Ralph Waldo Emerson once said, "The invariable mark of wisdom is to see the miraculous in the common." Perhaps one of the gifts of our crises is this wisdom. Our hearts, recognizing life is neither a permanent nor a trouble-free proposition, are quicker to connect with those who similarly struggle and with the beautiful complexity of the world around us.

- *Enhanced perspective on life and purpose.* Along with an awakening to life's beauty can come a reordering of priorities—a shift in our perspectives of what is truly important or worthy of our time. For me, I was stunned by the riches my close friends brought into my life through their wisdom, compassion, and support. I have described my sense of wonder at what they bring into my life as having a treasure box of precious stones. As I reflect on each of them, I glory in the beauty and differences in each jewel contained within. Close, intimate relationships with these women continue to be one of the beautiful gifts I cherish today.

After a challenging time has ended, when more energy and time are available, you may find yourself unwilling to return to your pre-crisis world. Family, time off, health, giving back to the community, and friends are some of the priorities clients have found more important after their difficult times.

We frequently don't value what seems endlessly available—money, time, family and friends, our health, or our days on this Earth. Having those things threatened or curtailed can bring a focus and appreciation to our perspectives. And when we look carefully at something we have taken for granted, we can find unexpected beauty in it.

These changes in how you view life can be deep and existential in nature. Not uncommonly, the crisis sets a process in place, a questioning about what is truly important, that creates an opening to other experiences which may continue to alter your path. While Nick had for years been intrigued by psychology, his interest in making a difference in individual lives came several years after he had finished his cancer treatment. Yet it was, I believe, in the hours he spent wondering about his own life and being the recipient of others' care that the seeds of his compassion and desire for service were planted.

- *Enhanced spiritual life.* Another domain in which existential shifts can occur is in the religious or spiritual beliefs you hold. Calhoun, Cann, Tedeschi, and McMillan found a significant relationship between post-traumatic growth and the willingness to allow the traumatic event to deepen or change one's spiritual belief.[30] While research[31] and my experience with clients suggest individuals who operate from a traditional religious framework may feel abandoned by a God who has allowed bad things to happen to them, there are a compelling number of others who find they feel connected and supported by their beliefs in new and profound ways they had never experienced before. As the crisis wanes, clients can report their faith feels stronger and more solid than before—that when everything else was being displaced in their lives, their religious or spiritual beliefs were an anchor they held on to. In fact, one of my clients, when I told him I was interviewing senior executives and their experiences with cancer for a future book, stated emphatically, "I don't know how you would get through something like that without a religious faith." And while a sizable number of people successfully go through a crisis without any sort of spiritual framework, those who have one may find that they have explored it and come to understand it differently than before. For example, sometimes they find themselves using words such as faith, solace, or grace more frequently. One of my especially practical clients surprised me when she admitted in a session, "This crisis has helped me to see the miracles in small things. It has sharpened my lens for grace." Grace has been a tricky word for me to define in my life. Anne Lamott's definition, in her book, *Help, Thanks, Wow: Three Essential Prayers,* resonated with me as I searched around for a way to understand it. Lamott writes "Grace can be the experience of a second wind, even though what you want is clarity and resolution, what you get is stamina, poignancy, and the strength to carry on." (p. 47) My experience has been that once your life has been touched by grace, in those moments when it feels like someone or something has your back, when everything else seems pretty crappy, you are changed in profound and lasting ways. Your view is altered and blink though you might, it's difficult to ever see in the old ways again.

Another friend, widowed about the same time I was, found her fairly traditional religious beliefs underwent a softening, perhaps in keeping with the compassion and empathy mentioned earlier. She found herself less willing to believe her church had the only answers, dooming those who didn't believe the same way to an eternity without grace. In our conversations since she has seemed more open to different viewpoints while still steadfast in her own.

If I were to sum up the factor connecting these areas for growth, it is perspective. It is impossible, I believe, to step back into the stream of life as the same person you were prior to the crisis. Seismic, traumatic events shake us and though we may, on the outside, look the same, we are different. And, while there may be a tremendous push by our families and friends for us to be who we were before the crisis, I don't perceive that as helpful or indeed possible. I have yet, in my conversations with clients or my experiences with individuals who have gone through difficult life challenges, found anyone who said they were unchanged by their crisis. It is, as stated before, up to us to decide how that change will impact us, our lives, and our relationships with others.

STRATEGY #3. RESPECT THE WOUNDS BUT LET THEM HEAL.

In addition to how we choose to perceive the impact of the crisis on our life, I believe everyone must decide the role this crisis will play in their lives and for how long. Nick made a conscious decision to tell none of his new friends at college, at least initially, about his cancer. It was a part of his life he was grateful to leave behind. When he began to work as a mental health associate in a residential treatment facility for adolescents, after graduating with a degree in social work and psychology, he found telling his story made more sense. The authenticity of his traumatic experiences provide him the necessary street credibility to create relationships with the youth who have also gone through trauma or at least serious challenges in their lives. And, with those experiences in common, Nick's advice and suggestions can found a more receptive place to land in adolescents who were more accustomed to tuning out adults.

Other clients, I have found, are unable to find their way out of the nightmare the crisis engendered in their lives. Despite the fact that the crisis is no longer active in their lives, they still live traumatized by the experience and its aftermath. Negative outcomes have defined them and painted a bleak life perspective. Sarah, a client whose daughter died tragically in a boating accident was able to find a way to live with the horrible loss but had to do so without her husband. Since their daughter's death, he spends his non-working hours drunk, withdrawn, or angry, unable to find his way out—neither his marriage or his relationship with his remaining children being sufficient impetus to seek help.

For me, this is the most heartbreaking work I do, for I continue to detect possibilities, growth and strengths where some of my clients see none. All I can do is honor their perspective and their pain, and be as helpful as I can as they make their ways through their never-ending stories. I believe sometimes they mistake reaching out for the possibilities of growth as denying their anguish. Or perhaps, as Caroline Myss suggests in *Why People Don't Heal and How They Can*, we have become a culture of "woundology" holding on tightly or overly long to our wounds because we believe they define us or allow us some special privileges, perhaps of sympathy or accommodation. The wounds can also be a way to stay in denial, to refuse to move on to a life beyond the crisis. As my client Bridget wrote in her email to me, "Rage allowed me to ignore my life's next chapter. Like a sponge it (rage) absorbed me; I was too consumed with keeping it secret to wring it dry."

And yet, the research on post-traumatic growth, as well as my experiences with crisis, trauma, and torture survivors who have found optimism, indicate that growth does not mean forgetting the pain. Instead it is unearthing a way to find the goodness in life despite it.

Studies have explored the experiences of individuals who have experienced post-traumatic growth after disruptive (Calhoun and Tedeschi use the term "seismic") events.[32] Common negative outcomes include a loss of security and a knowledge that both they and their lives are less durable than they believed before. A friend lost his beloved wife merely ten days after she was diagnosed with a rapidly spreading cancer. When I flew down to be with him as he sorted through her belongings and his thoughts, he kept saying, over and over, "I just didn't realize how fragile she was." For him life had become more tenuous than he had known it to be before the loss of his love.

It is a hard balance, allowing ourselves to grieve the loss of a loved one or a potential, perhaps expected future, and recognizing when we have lost our way in the process and let our wounds dictate our life. And while some of the effects of trauma will not disappear solely because you wish them to, you may want to consider engaging a counselor or other mental health professional to help you disengage from the cold comfort of that hurt, if you find yourself hanging on to it. This is particularly true if you continue to experience some of the more intense symptoms of trauma after the crisis has ended (see "The First Stage: Surviving the Initial Shock").

I, like Caroline Myss, believe we have far more choices, perhaps responsibilities, in how we deal with our challenges. Myss, a best-selling author and speaker on human consciousness, spirituality, health, and energy medicine, puts it eloquently in *Why People Don't Heal and How They Can*: "We are not meant to stay wounded," she writes. "We are supposed to move through our tragedies and challenges and help others move through the many painful episodes of our lives. By remaining stuck in the power of our wounds we block our own transformation. We overlook the larger gifts inherent in our wounds—the strength to overcome them and the lessons we are meant to receive through them. Wounds are the means through which we enter the hearts of other people. They are meant to teach us to become passionate and wise." (p.15)

CHAPTER 2:
CLAIM THE GOLD AND PASS IT ON

Something is going to come out of this, something new. This can end you up in a whole new place, a better place, a much more open place.
–Maya Angelou

One day while Vito was in the hospital, Nick and I had to go get his driver's license renewed. As we stood in line, we saw the dad of one of his friends. Anil appeared haggard and thinner than we had seen him last, with less bounce and optimism than his usual demeanor. In sorrowful tones he announced to us he had recently been diagnosed with chronic obstructive pulmonary disease and learning to live with the disease had been a real challenge for him. He went into some detail about the impact the diagnosis had had on his sense of trust in the Universe and his own health.

Nick and I looked at each other—only a quick glance, but it was enough. Silently, we made the decision not to share our news. It would sound a little bit, at least to our ears, as crisis one-upmanship. "I'll take your disease, and raise you cancer and GBS." Caught up in his own misery, he didn't press us much for news about our world and so, with our hopes for safe passage through his crisis and our love to his family, we went on our way. We served him best by standing witness to where he was, not where we were. And, in that moment of clarity, Nick and I both began to integrate what we had learned about compassion, perspective, and living more purposefully into our lives.

STRATEGIES

STRATEGY #1. RECOGNIZE AND NURTURE YOUR WISDOM.

I've taught workshops around the world for over thirty years, on a variety of topics ranging from interpersonal skills to change management to strategic thinking. Invariably the workshops are filled to the brim with exercises, readings, skill practices, and discussions; it is significantly more data than most people can process. So my fellow trainers and I typically would end the workshop by asking each of the participants to talk about what they would actually put into practice at work once they returned to their normal lives. Because most classes ended on a Friday, we called the final exercise **What I Shall Do On M**onday or WISDOM. One by one our participants would stand up and name the one or two ideas or exercises which had stuck with them—the *aha* moment that had occurred. The WISDOM reports I loved hearing the most were the ones where they were choosing to take on something with personal meaning for them—having the difficult conversations earlier, not multi-tasking when a direct report came into their office, asking more questions instead of assuming they already had the answers. I knew that if they used only one WISDOM idea, their lives would benefit as would those of the people around them. Some ideas to recognize your wisdom:

- What have you learned that others could benefit from?

- What will you do differently, should another crisis arise in your life?

- What have you seen about yourself, your values, your purpose that can never be "unseen"?

There is also a discontinuous quality to integrating the changes into your life. Sometimes, we start with small shifts—exercising more, leaving work earlier, volunteering to help someone in need, adding a centering prayer or meditation to our morning ritual—but as our lives continue, those small changes can yield larger ones, and then still more profound ones, until the life we are living looks little like the one we had in the days before the crisis. One of my clients made a commitment to himself to stop his numbing behaviors (drinking excessively and mindlessly eating) once his wife was in recovery from multiple medical crises. As Jack has struggled to keep his commitment, his lifelong fear of facing his feelings surfaced. As he began to address his deeply buried feelings, powerful insights and unexpected (and rocky) spurts of progress have occurred for him. He surprised me one day when he texted me to let me know he had decided feelings weren't such a bad thing; they were data. This was a quite a surprise coming from a man who had told me on numerous occasions he *"hated"* feelings! I quickly texted back, "Who are you and what have you done with my client?" It was an incredible shift for him.

Nurturing the change means finding ways to support the new perspectives you have gained and taking actions in line with who you are and are becoming. By nurturing yourself and sharing what you have learned with others, you both claim and integrate the ways in which this crisis has changed you for the better.

STRATEGY #2. FIND YOUR TRIBE.

This entails locating a supportive community of like-minded people who are on a similar path to discovery or service. Meet-ups (web sites which serve as notice boards for people who come together around particular topics such as wine tasting, martial arts, or volunteer service), church groups, online workshops, retreats, and book clubs are some of the ways to find people to walk alongside you as you make the journey forward. As I mentioned previously, post-crisis you may have some different perspectives or interests. Finding a group of people who will share those and encourage you can make integrating them into your life easier.

My client Claire is a lawyer, a cancer survivor, and had recently divorced when she came to therapy. She was still trying to make sense of the disappointments and difficulties in her life while supporting her son who was recovering from a serious accident a few years earlier. Struggling with the challenges of being female in a male-dominated area of the law, she decided to take a six-week Internet course that explored women's authentic power. The course was designed to help women understand their gifts and purpose, as well as to encourage their strengths and wisdom. Exhilarated and challenged by the exercises, she found a low-key way to interact with others who were looking to make similar changes in their lives.

STRATEGY #3. SHARE WHAT YOU HAVE LEARNED.

Another way to integrate the changes into your life is to pass on your wisdom. As anyone who has ever taught a class knows, the best way to learn something is to have to share it with another (or a class of senior executives!). In telling others our story, we continue to crystallize it for ourselves. This doesn't mean buttonholing people at parties to tell them what you've learned and what they should do differently, obviously, but it may mean looking for opportunities to offer your knowledge, if someone is interested. I recently met an extremely successful but introverted executive recently who had tragically lost a daughter to suicide. Since her daughter's death, Jo Ann has quietly informed her church she is available to help parents who have lost a child. As Jo Ann said, in her quiet, understated way, "I'm not qualified to talk to people about most experiences of loss, but this one, I can."

Some clients feel driven to share what they've learned in order to spare others the same trauma. One gentleman, Keith, after going through prostate cancer, has taken every opportunity offered to him (and created considerable more) to talk to men about getting their prostates checked. He routinely asks his male friends if they "know their numbers" and encourages them to visit a doctor if they haven't. Keith feels like his discussions are both a form of service and of gratitude for the gift he was given of life.

Others who have suffered through a crisis have gone on to create foundations. The V foundation (www.jimmyv.org), created by Jim Valvano (the beloved basketball coach who led his North Carolina State University team to a NCAA championship before becoming a well-known sportscaster for ESPN), is a striking example of the creation of someone who was determined to forge purpose from the tragedy in his life. When Valvano was diagnosed with metastatic adenocarcinoma, his focus turned to helping others with cancer. With help from ESPN and innumerable others, he founded the V Foundation, designed to fund cancer research. His legacy has awarded more than $130 million in funds to over 120 facilities engaged in the fight against the disease that took his life. In one of the last interviews he gave he said, "I want to help every cancer patient I can now. I don't know if I can handle that, but it's the only conceivable good that can come out of this."

Late in 2013, Benjamin LeRoy, a writer and the publisher of Tyrus Books, lost a close friend to suicide. After reading the farewell note his friend left behind, in which he discussed his attempt to find purpose through serving others, Benjamin set out across America to do volunteer work in all fifty states over the course of twelve months in order to honor his friend's legacy and to better understand his role in the world. Another friend, having lost her son to suicide as well, set up a scholarship program in her late child's name.

School shootings, serious health crises, mental illnesses, sexual assaults, homelessness, war, natural disasters, and violence are among the serious life challenges or traumas to serve as unlikely spring-boards for those who want to create good from their pain. The point is not how people have chosen to pay tribute to the new awareness their crisis has brought them, whether it's in subtle ways or on a grand scale, but rather that they've recognized within themselves the power to use the tough times they've faced to assist others.

Frankl provides a powerful example of an individual who decided a severely traumatic experience would not break him, but instead serve as a launching pad to help others. After his three years in various concentration camps where he lost almost every member of his family, including his wife, Frankl counseled other survivors, remarried, taught at prestigious universities, lectured across the world, published thirty-nine books, received countless awards, earned a Ph.D. in philosophy, and became known as the founder of a branch of psychology known as logotherapy. Throughout his life, Frankl affirmed his beliefs that humans have the freedom to choose how they will respond to the events in their lives, that finding meaning was a primary motivation for humans, and that bringing forth the best in oneself is part of the freedom and the responsibility everyone shares. His most well-known book, *Man's Search for Meaning,* is considered one of the most influential books of all time. Its original title, translated from German, perhaps speaks most eloquently of what he learned from tragedy. The title was, *Saying Yes to Life in Spite of Everything: A Psychologist Experiences the Concentration Camp.*

Regardless of how you choose to view the challenge you have gone through and what to do with the nuggets of gold you may have found in its wake, there is a ripple effect initiated by a crisis in your life. You are different now than you were before. The shift will unfold in ways both visible and unseen. Sometimes the first waves flowing out from a crisis are small—a tattoo, like Nick's, that says, "Never Give Up;" more patience with a child's antics; a new openness to emotional intimacy; an appreciation for a day without pain or for the medical professionals who cared for you; a sense of responsibility in helping others through similar challenges. The undulations caused by those first ripples continue to play out into our lives—reprioritizing the work we do or the time we spend with family, making boundaries easier to set and keep, shifting our focus, perhaps, to something bigger than our own lives. For me, writing this book based on what I learned has led me to wonder how business people, at the tops of their careers, cope with traumas such as cancer. That research is the basis of the book I am now writing, called *The Wisdom of Cancer* (working title).

Similarly, the wounding of our spirits and our bodies can also unfold from those events, shifting our views of life, our senses of possibilities, or our willingness to venture outside of ourselves. And although we may not have had any choice in some of the harm that came our way, we still have one critical decision to make—how we will let it change us.

ENDING THOUGHTS

*In the midst of winter, I found there was, within me,
an invincible summer. And that makes me happy. For it
says that no matter how hard the world pushes against
me, within me, there's something stronger—something
better, pushing right back.*
–Albert Camus

I believe those of us who have gone through serious hardships be-come, in some cosmic way, related. We form a tribe of battle veter-ans and fellow pilgrims suffused with knowledge none of us wanted. And although the admission to the club is unexpected and painful, the people you meet once you are there and the person you become will be with you forever.

My intent on this journey through *The Gift of Crisis* was to walk alongside of you, making your path a little less frightening, a touch more manageable. And as you find your way out of this hardship, I hope you will recognize the gold you earned as you went through the crucible of crisis. The strengths you found, the compassion that emerged, the shifting of priorities—they are uniquely yours. If you have found something valuable, it is my hope you will chose to pass it on or share it with those who are standing at the beginning of their journey, looking shell-shocked and afraid.

I do feel impelled to share with you what I have learned, that having gone through a crisis doesn't prevent future challenges from visiting you. I am still bemused by the opportunities for growth continuing to arrive in my life—or as I like to call them—AFGOs (another frickin' growth opportunity). More and more I recognize them as ways my soul is lightening its load of the debris this life has accumulated around it. Regardless, though, of where the AFGOs take me, I have come to perceive that I am not alone—not for an instant. I have learned the hard way that, when fear or challenge stands in the middle of the road, daring me to take it on, Divine assistance is at work in my life—whether or not I sense Its presence. And I have found the best response to tough times is to say "thank you"—even when I don't know yet why I will be grateful.

I wanted a perfect ending. Now I've learned, the hard way, that some poems don't rhyme, and some stories don't have a clear beginning, middle, and end. Life is about not knowing, having to change, taking the moment and making the best of it, without knowing what's going to happen next.

–Gilda Radner
June 28, 1946—May 20, 1989

APPENDIX A

QUESTIONS TO HELP YOU TELL YOUR STORY:

- When and how did the crisis begin? Was it unexpected or did you see it coming?

- What were your reactions? How did you feel physically? What emotions seemed most prevalent? What were your initial thoughts?

- How did you get through those first few days? What seemed to work for you? What comforted you?

- When did you recognize you were ready to move forward into action?

- What helped you regain your balance, your sense of perspective? Were there any intentions you set for yourself?

- What was important to you about how you handled yourself during the first part of the crisis? Were there any long-held values that became more important? Did any long-term beliefs or values seem no longer relevant?

- Who was there for you? Were you surprised by anything in terms of the support you received or didn't receive from family, friends, and others?

- What were the worst parts of the crisis for you? Were there any times that scared you or caused great anxiety in you?

- How did you handle the worst parts of this crisis?

- What were your coping strategies? For example, did you compartmentalize, reach out to friends, refuse to dwell on it, sleep or eat more than usual, exercise? What seemed to help? What worked against you?

- Did you find yourself saying or doing anything that was unusual for you? Was it helpful or not?

- When things began to settle down, did you have to let go of any parts of your usual life in order to make things function? When did you realize that the old ways of doing things would no longer work for you? What did you do instead, when the old ways no longer fit?

- What was the hardest to let go of? What did you lose that you still grieve for or find upsetting? Are you looking for ways to replace what you have lost? If so, what are they?

- How did you "make it all work"? What were some of the strategies that suited you? What were some which didn't?

- What skills or strengths did you find within yourself you weren't aware you possessed?

- Were there any surprising weaknesses or vulnerabilities that arose?

- What did friends or family members say about you during the crisis?

- What are some of the emotions you remember feeling most consistently?

- Did you develop any helpful rituals or patterns to it through the ordeal? Will you bring any of those with you into the future? Which ones are you ready to discard?

- Were there sayings, scriptures, affirmations, or symbols that gave you courage, a sense of peace, or help in some way?

- Did your connection to your spiritual life change in any way during the crisis? If so, how?

APPENDIX B

QUESTIONS TO HELP CLARIFY YOUR THOUGHTS:

- What outcome would please you the most?

- What is your intuition telling you?

- How will your choices affect others? How are you being affected right now?

- What have you tried so far? What happened when you did that?

- What are your reasons or thoughts regarding the situation?

- What do you believe is the core problem? Are there other issues impacting this?

- As you've tried something, when is it better? When is it worse?

- What additional information do you need? Where can you get it?

- Who else can you trust to help you reason this through?

- Is there anyone else who will be impacted by this decision?

- Who do you want to include or exclude from the conversation for the moment?

- Is anyone or anything getting in the way of your preferred course of action?

- By when do you need to decide? Is this your timetable or someone else's?

- What can others do to be of help to you now?

- When and how will you ask for for assistance?

ACKNOWLEDGMENTS

This book has been shepherded and nurtured into existence by an extraordinary community of support for which I am both grateful and amazed. It wouldn't have been written except for the courageous journeys of my two men, my son Nick and my late husband Vito. Their resilience, humor, and bravery were my inspiration and my motivation during the three years our family fought one serious medical crisis after another.

Alongside of me during those years were my family—loving, present, and accepting. They bombarded the Heavens with prayers I believe were behind more than one miracle. Then they showed up to help. I feel very lucky to have my family. They have gone through their own crises during these years. Their resilience, love, and faith inspired and supported my path as I wrote this book.

The support of close friends, wise medical professionals, and an extraordinary company, Personnel Decisions International (now PDI Korn Ferry), made the journey through those crisis years possible. Thank you especially to Brenda Parker, Dr. Jason Litten, the 10th floor nurses at Children's Medical Center in Dallas, and my colleagues at PDI.

The community of friends who have been part of my team from the beginning have their "sticky fingers" (thank you for that term, Barbara Lavery) all over this book. Some, like Barbara and Jo Waller, were the (unpaid) editors on my first iteration of my book – keeping me on track, asking loving questions, and offering great feedback. Dr. Craig Hurwitz looked it over for me as well – bringing both his compassion and pediatric oncology and palliative care expertise to the process. Ann Radebaugh brought the experience of her many years as an English teacher while Sharon Galbreath contributed her detail orientation and incredible focus to the first iteration of this book.

Throughout the multiple versions of *The Gift of Crisis*, other friends have freely contributed their expert knowledge, ideas, and encouragement: Susan Braun, Diane Marentette, Bobbie Little, Brigitte Iafrate, Michelle Bardwell, Maryann Russell, Patrick Lavery, Karen James, and Larry Pile. *The Gift of Crisis* wouldn't be here without them. Thank you as well to the clients who chose to share their stories and their wisdom. I am constantly awed by the bravery of the people I am privileged to work with in my practices.

Robyn Russell, my editor, brought graceful interventions--expertise, wise suggestions, and humor allowing my book to find its way. Thank you, also, to Jason Buchholz, as well as Kate Sciolino and Kelly Notaras, from the awesome KN Literary agency.

In its final editing, my dear friend and gifted intuitive adviser, Maryann Russell and the "Greek Council" (you know who you are), brought their wisdom and blessings to this book. Thank you, thank you, thank you!

RESOURCES

The books and healing ideas listed here are based on my own experiences and preferences. The suggestions with regard to alternative healing are based on my limited knowledge and personal preferences. They should be pursued only after talking to a trusted medical professional.

POST-TRAUMATIC GROWTH

Calhoun, Lawrence, and Tedeschi, Richard. Facilitating Posttraumatic Growth: A Clinician's Guide. New York, NY: Routledge, 1999.

Calhoun, Lawrence et al. A Correlational Test of the Relationship Between Posttraumatic Growth, Religion, and Cognitive Processing. Journal of Traumatic Stress, 13 (3), 521-527. 2000

Joseph, Stephen and Linley, P. Alex. Trauma, Recovery, and Growth: Positive Psychological Perspectives on Posttraumatic Stress. Hoboken, NJH: Wiley, 2010.

Lesser, Elizabeth. Broken Open: How Difficult Times Can Help Us Grow. New York, NY: Villard, 2005.

Orloff, Judith. Positive Energy: 10 Extraordinary Prescriptions for Transforming Fatigue, Stress, and Fear into Vibrance, Strength, and Love. New York: Harmony Books, 2004.

HANDLING STRESS, FEAR, AND ANXIETY

Chödrön, Pema. The Places That Scare You: a Guide to Fearlessness in Difficult Times. Boston: Shambhala, 2002.

Conway, Diane. What Would You Do If You Had No Fear? Living Your Dreams While Quakin' in Your Boots. Makawao, HI: Inner Ocean Publishing, 2004.

Dossey, Larry. Reinventing Medicine: Beyond Mind-Body to a New Era of Healing. New York, NY: HarperCollins, 1999.

Hanson, Rick, and Richard Mendius. Buddha's Brain: the Practical Neuro-science of Happiness, Love and Wisdom. Oakland, CA: New Harbinger Publications, 2009.

Kabat-Zinn, Jon. Full Catastrophe Living: Using the Wisdom of Your Body and Mind to Face Stress, Pain, and Illness. New York, NY: Pub. by Dell Pub., a Division of Bantam Doubleday Dell Pub. Group, 1991.

Katie, Byron, and Stephen Mitchell. Loving What Is: Four Questions That Can Change Your Life. New York: Harmony Books, 2002.

Lerner, Harriet Goldhor. Fear and Other Uninvited Guests: Tackling the Anxiety, Fear, and Shame That Keep Us from Optimal Living and Loving. New York: HarperCollins Publishers, 2004.

Moore, Thomas. Dark Nights of the Soul: A Guide to Finding Your Way Through Life's Ordeals. New York, NY: Gotham Books, 2004.

Orloff, Judith. Second Sight. New York: Warner Books, 1996.

Orloff, Judith. The Ecstasy of Surrender: 12 Surprising Ways Letting Go Can Empower Your Life. New York: HarmonyBooks, 2014.

Pennebaker, James. Opening Up: The Healing Power of Expressing Emotions. New York: The Guilford Press. 1990.

STAYING PRESENT AND GROUNDED

Frankl, Viktor. Man's Search for Meaning. Boston, MA: Beacon Press, 1959.

Hanson, Rick, and Richard Mendius. Buddha's Brain: the Practical Neuro-science of Happiness, Love and Wisdom. Oakland, CA: New Harbinger Publications, 2009.

Tolle, Eckhart. The Power of Now: A Guide to Spiritual Enlightenment. Novato, CA: New World Library, 1999.

Whiteman, Honor. "Social Media: How Does It Really Affect Our Mental Health and Well-Being?" Medical News Today: n. pag. Web. April 16, 2014.

MANAGING THE MIND MONKEYS

Basco, Monica Ramirez. Never Good Enough: Freeing Yourself From the Chains of Perfectionism. New York: Free Press, 1999.

Brown, C. Brené. The Gifts of Imperfection: Let Go of Who You Think You're Supposed to Be and Embrace Who You Are. Center City, MN: Hazelden, 2010.

Katie, Byron, and Stephen Mitchell. A Thousand Names for Joy: Living in Harmony with the Way Things Are. New York: Harmony Books, 2007.

Kayany, Joseph M. "Information Overload and Information Myths." *Information and Telecommunications Education and Research Association:* n. pag. n. d. Web.

Singer, Michael A. The Untethered Soul: The Journey Beyond Yourself. Oakland, CA: New Harbinger Press, 2007.

SELF-NURTURING

Ford, Debbie. The Dark Side of the Light Chasers. New York: Riverhead Books, 1998.

Imber-Black, Evan and Roberts, Janine. Rituals For Our Times; Celebrating, Healing, and Changing Our Lives and Our Relationships. New York, NY: HarperCollins, 1992.

Lamott, Anne. Traveling Mercies: Some Thoughts on Faith. New York, NY: Anchor Books, 1999.

Loehr, James E., and Tony Schwartz. The Power of Full Engagement: Managing Energy, Not Time, Is the Key to High Performance and Personal Renewal. New York: Free Press, 2003.

Domar, Alice D., and Henry Dreher. Self-Nurture: Learning to Care for Yourself as Effectively as You Care for Everyone Else. New York: Viking Penguin, 2000.

Schaef, Anne Wilson. Meditations for Women Who Do Too Much. New York, NY: HarperCollins, 1990.

Shimoff, Marci. Happy for No Reason: 7 Steps to Being Happy From the Inside Out. New York: Free Press, 2008.

"Stress Relief From Laughter? It's No Joke." *MayoClinic.org*. Mayo Foundation for Medical Education and Research, July 23, 2013. Web. May 16, 2015.

Trafton, Richard S. and Marentette, S. Diane. A New Brain for Business. San Diego, CA: New Brain for Business Institute, 2010.

Viorst, Judith. Necessary Losses: The Loves, Illusions, Dependencies, and Impossible Expectations that All of Us Have to Give Up in Order to Grow. New York, NY: Fireside, 1986.

Williamson, Gay and Williamson, David. Transformative Rituals: Celebrations for Personal Growth. Deerfield Beach, FL: HCI Books, 1994.

BEING INTENTIONAL

Buckingham, Marcus. Go Put Your Strengths to Work: 6 Powerful Steps to Achieve Outstanding Performance. New York: Free Press, 2007.

Day, Laura. Welcome to Your Crisis: How to Use the Power of Crisis to Create the Life You Want. New York: Little, Brown and Company, 2006.

Dossey, Larry. Healing Words: the Power of Prayer and the Practice of Medicine. San Francisco, CA: HarperSanFrancisco, 1993.

Dyer, Wayne W. The Power of Intention: Learning to Co-Create Your World Your Way. Carlsbad, CA: Hay House, 2004.

Emmons, Robert. "10 Ways to Become More Grateful." GreaterGood.Berkeley.edu. The Greater Good Science Center at the University of California, Berkeley, November 17, 2010. Web. May 16, 2015.

Katherine, Anne. Boundaries: Where You End and I Begin. Park Ridge, IL: Parkside Pub., 1991.

Kornfield, Jack. The Art of Forgiveness, Lovingkindness, and Peace. New York: Bantam Books, 2002.

McTaggart, Lynne. The Intention Experiment: Using Your Thoughts to Change Your Life and the World. New York: Free Press, 2007.

Muller, Wayne. How, Then, Shall We Live?: Four Simple Questions That Reveal the Beauty and Meaning of Our Lives. New York: Bantam Books, 1996.

Ruge, Kenneth. Where Do I Go From Here? An Inspirational Guide to Making Authentic Career and Life Choices. New York, NY: McGraw-Hill, 1998.

Schultz, Mona Lisa. Awakening Intuition: Using Your Mind-Body Network for Insight and Healing. New York, NY: Three Rivers Press, 1998.

AFFIRMATIONS

Ponder, Catherine. The Dynamic Laws of Healing. Camarillo, CA: DeVorss Publications, 1966.

VISUALIZATION

Naparstek, Belleruth. Staying Well with Guided Imagery. New York: Warner Books, 1994.

Siegel, Bernie S. Peace, Love & Healing: Bodymind Communication and the Path to Self-Healing: An Exploration. New York: Harper & Row, 1989.

THE POWER OF JOURNALING

Baldwin, Christina. Life's Companion: Journal Writing as a Spiritual Practice. New York: Bantam Books, 1990.

Cameron, Julia. The Artist's Way: A Spiritual Path to Higher Creativity. New York: Tarcher/Putnam, 1992.

Pennebaker, James. Writing to Heal: A Guided Journal for Recovering From Trauma & Emotional Upheaval. Oakland, CA: New Harbinger Publications, 2004.

Pennebaker, James and Evans, John. Expressive Writing: Words That Heal. Enumclaw, WA: Idyll Arbor, 2014.

Smyth, J. M. Written Emotional Expression: Effect Size, Outcome Types, and Moderating Variables. Manuscript submitted for publication, 1996.

LEVERAGING YOUR STRENGTHS

Covey, Stephen R. The 7 Habits of Highly Effective People: Powerful Lessons in Personal Change. New York, NY: Simon & Schuster, 1989.

Kaplan, Robert E. and Kaiser, Robert B. "Stop Overdoing Your Strengths." HBR.org. Harvard Business Review, Feb. 2009. Web. May 16, 2015.

Rath, Tom. Strengthsfinder 2.0. New York, NY: Gallup Press, 2007.

COPING WITH A SERIOUS ILLNESS

Bolen, Jean Shinoda. Close to the Bone: Life-Threatening Illness and the Search for Meaning. New York: Scribner, 1996.

Lerner, Michael. Choices in Healing: Integrating the Best of Conventional and Complementary Approaches to Cancer. Cambridge, MA: MIT Press, 1996.

Kushner, Harold S. When Bad Things Happen to Good People. New York, NY: Avon Books, 1981.

Halpern, Susan P. The Etiquette of Illness: What to Say When You Can't Find the Words. New York: Bloomsbury, 2004.

Myss, Caroline. Why People Don't Heal and How They Can. New York, NY: Three Rivers Press, 1997.

Ram, Dass, Mark Matousek, and Marlene Roeder. Still Here: Embracing Aging, Changing, and Dying. New York: Riverhead Books, 2000.

Remen, Rachel Naomi. Kitchen Table Wisdom: Stories That Heal. New York: Riverhead Books, 2006.

THOUGHTS AND RESOURCES ON GRIEF, DEATH AND DYING

Jamison, Stephen. Final Acts of Love: Families, Friends, and Assisted Dying. New York: G.P. Putnam's Sons, 1995.

Kubler-Ross, Elisabeth, and Kessler, David. On Grief and Grieving: Finding the Meaning of Grief Through the Five Stages of Loss. New York, NY: Scribner, 2005.

Levine, Stephen. Meetings at the Edge: Dialogues with the Grieving and the Dying, the Healing and the Healed. Garden City, NY: Anchor Press, 1984.

Nuland, Sherwin B. How We Die: Reflections on Life's Final Chapter. New York: Vintage Books, 2010.

Spiegel, David. Living Beyond Limits: New Hope and Help for Facing Life-Threatening Illness. New York: Times Books, 1993.

CREATING THE LIFE YOU WANT

Attwood, Janet Bray., and Chris Attwood. The Passion Test: the Effortless Path to Discovering Your Destiny. New York: Hudson Street Press, 2007.

Beck, Martha Nibley. The Joy Diet: 10 Daily Practices for a Happier Life. New York: Crown Publishers, 2003.

Chapman, Gary D. The 5 Love Languages: The Secret to Love that Lasts. Oakland, CA: New Harbinger Press, 2007.

Dalai Lama, HH, and Howard C. Cutler. The Art of Happiness: a Handbook for Living. New York: Riverhead Books, 1998.

Farmer, Steven. Animal Spirit Guides: An Easy-to-Use Handbook for Identifying and Understanding Your Power Animals and Animal Spirit Helpers. Carlsbad, CA: Hay House, 2006.

Ford, Debbie. The Right Questions: Ten Essential Questions to Guide You to an Extraordinary Life. San Francisco: HarperSanFrancisco, 2003.

Lawlor, Anthony. The Temple in the House: Finding the Sacred in Everyday Architecture. New York: Putnam, 1994.

Leider, Richard, and David A. Shapiro. Repacking Your Bags: How to Live with a New Sense of Purpose. New York: MJF Books, 1996.

Levoy, Gregg. Callings: Finding and Following an Authentic Life. New York: Random House of Canada, 1998.

Richardson, Cheryl. Take Time for Your Life: a Personal Coach's Seven-Step Program for Creating the Life You Want. New York: Broadway Books, 1999.

Virtue, Doreen. Angel Therapy. Carlsbad, CA: Hay House, 2011.

Virtue, Doreen. Angels 101: An Introduction to Connecting, Working, and Healing with the Angels. Carlsbad, CA: Hay House, 2006.

Virtue, Doreen. The Lightworker's Way: Awakening Your Spiritual Power to Know and Heal. Carlsbad, CA: Hay House, 1997.

Virtue, Doreen, and Brown, Lynette. Angel Numbers 101: The Meaning of 111, 123, 444, and Other Number Sequences. Carlsbad, CA: Hay House, 2005.

ALTERNATIVE HEALING IDEAS

Massage: Massages are a deeply relaxing and helpful way to release tension. Recommendations from friends are one of the best ways to find a good masseuse. Some guidelines to having a great massage include:

- Check to make sure that your masseuse is board-certified. This establishes a level of both professionalism and training.

- Talk about what kind of massage you want and the purpose for which you are getting it—to relax, to work out muscle tension, to energize you.

- Communicate during the massage about how the amount of pressure is feeling to you. Don't assume that the therapist knows.

- Let the therapist know if you want them to interact with you or not. Some people like silence and others enjoy talking.

- If anything feels uncomfortable to you or you don't like the way you are being touched, speak up immediately. A good masseuse will be want to be told.

Websites about massage:

- www.massagetherapy.com (a public education site sponsored by Bodywork and massage professionals)
- altmedicine.about.com/od/massage/Massage_Therapy.htm (About.com's explanation and FAQs on massage)

Reiki: Reiki is a form of energy healing that does not require touching, although some practitioners do use their hands at certain points in the session. For some people, it is as soothing and relaxing as massage, if not more. Additional information:

- There are three levels of Reiki training; check to find out which level your practitioner has—level three is the most skilled and, in my opinion, preferable.

- Again, recommendations from friends are the best way to find skilled Reiki practitioners. You can also Google Reiki in your city/hometown.

- Be sure to check their credentials and ask for a recommendation from a client if you don't have a personal recommendation to go on.

Websites about Reiki:

- www.reiki.org (sponsored by the International Center for Reiki training)
- healing.about.com/cs/reiki/a/reikiFAQ.htm (About.com's explanation and FAQs on Reiki)

AROMATHERAPY:

- Fischer-Rizzi, Susanne. Complete Aromatherapy Handbook: Essential Oils for Radiant Health. New York: Sterling Pub., 1990.

- Worwood, Valerie Ann. The Complete Book of Essential Oils and Aromatherapy. San Rafael, CA: New World Library, 1991.

ABOUT THE AUTHOR

Psychologist, author, speaker, and organizational consultant, Dr. Susan Mecca has worked with companies, families, couples, and individuals facing difficult and life-threatening challenges for over 35 years. In *The Gift of Crisis: Finding your best self in the worst of times* Dr. Mecca shares her clinical expertise, client stories, first-hand experiences as her son's and her husband's caregiver as well as current research on trauma, resilience, and post-traumatic growth.

If you found this book helpful, would you consider writing a review? Thank you!

For the latest news, book details, Susan's blog, or information about contacting Susan for speaking engagements, check out her website at www.drsusanmecca.com

ENDNOTES

[1] Mieli, The Finnish Association for Mental Health. Traumatic Crises. Retrieved from www.mielenterveysseura.fi/en/home/mental-health/crises/traumatic-crises

[2] Bridges, W. (2003). Managing Transitions: Making the Most of Change. Cambridge: Da Capo Press

[3] Personal correspondence with Michelle Bardwell, RA, www.flowerroad.net.

[4] Lieberman, M. D., Eisenberger, N. I., Crockett, M. J., Tom, S. M., Pfeifer, J. H., & Way, B. M. (2007). Putting Feelings into Words Affect Labeling Disrupts Amygdala Activity in Response to Affective Stimuli. Psychological science, 18(5), 421-428.

[5] Gotink, R. A., Hermans, K. S. F. M., Geschwind, N., De Nooij, R., De Groot, W. T., & Speckens, A. E. M. (2016). Mindfulness and Mood Stimulate Each Other in an Upward Spiral: A Mindful Walking Intervention Using Experience Sampling. Mindfulness, 7(5), 1114–1122. doi.org/10.1007/s12671-016-0550-8

[6] www.psychologicalscience.org/news/releases/stress-changes-how-people-make-decisions.html#.WHEFC7YrL-Y

[7] Gotay CC, Muraoka MY. Quality of Life in Long-Term Survivors of Adult-Onset Cancers. J Natl Cancer Inst. 1998;90:656–67.

[8] Dunkel-Schetter C. Social Support and Cancer: Findings Based on Patient Interviews and Their Implications. Journal of Social Issues. 1984;40:77–98.

[9] Danhauer, S. C., Case, L. D., Tedeschi, R., Russell, G., Vishnevsky, T., Triplett, K.,…Avis, N. E. (2013). Predictors of Posttraumatic Growth in Women with Breast Cancer. Psycho-Oncology, 22(12), 10.1002/pon.3298. doi.org/10.1002/pon.3298

[10] Ozbay, F., Johnson, D. C., Dimoulas, E., Morgan, C. A., Charney, D., & Southwick, S. (2007). Social Support and Resilience to Stress: From Neurobiology to Clinical Practice. Psychiatry (Edgmont), 4(5), 35–40.

[11] Ozbay, F., Johnson, D. C., Dimoulas, E., Morgan, C. A., Charney, D., & Southwick, S. (2007). Social Support and Resilience to Stress: From Neurobiology to Clinical Practice. Psychiatry (Edgmont), 4(5), 35–40.

[12] Bremner, J. D. (2006). Traumatic Stress: Effects on the Brain. Dialogues in Clinical Neuroscience, 8(4), 445–461.

[13] Kaplan, Robert E., and Robert B. Kaiser. "Stop Overdoing Your Strengths." Harvard Business Review. EBSCOhost, Feb. 2009. Web. 9 Jan. 2017

[14] Kayany, J. M. (2012). Information Overload and Information Myths. Itera, nd, www.itera.org/wordpress/wp-content/uploads,9,353-70.

[15] Krasnova, Hanna, et al. "Envy on Facebook: A Hidden Threat to Users' Life Satisfaction?" Wirtschaftsinformatik 92 (2013): 1-16.

[16] Przybylski, A. K., Murayama, K., DeHaan, C. R., & Gladwell, V. (2013). Motivational, emotional, and behavioral correlates of fear of missing out. Computers in Human Behavior, 29(4), 1841-1848.

ENDNOTES

[17] Smyth, J. M. (1998). Written emotional expression: effect sizes, outcome types, and moderating variables. Journal of consulting and clinical psychology, 66(1), 174.

[18] J. David Creswell, Janine M. Dutcher, William M. P. Klein, Peter R. Harris, John M. Levine. Self-Affirmation Improves Problem-Solving under Stress. PLoS ONE, 2013; 8 (5): e62593.

[19] Cohen, G. L., & Sherman, D. K. (2014). The Psychology of Change: Self-Affirmation and Social Psychological Intervention. Annual Review of Psychology, 65, 333-371.

[20] juliacameronlive.com/basic-tools/artists-dates

[21] Berry, D. S., & Pennebaker, J. W. (1993). Nonverbal and Verbal Emotional Expression and Health. Psychotherapy and Psychosomatics, 59(1), 11-19.

[22] Brown, Brené. Daring Greatly: How the Courage to Be Vulnerable Transforms the Way We Live, Love, Parent, and Lead. Penguin, 2012.

[23] Wientjes, K. A. Mind-Body Techniques in Wound Healing. Ostomy/wound Management, Vol 48, 11, 2002, pp62-67.

[24] Baird, C. L., and Sands, L. A Pilot Study of the Effectiveness of Guided Imagery with Progressive Muscle Relaxation to Reduce Chronic Pain and Mobility Difficulties of Osteoarthritis. Pain Management Nursing, Vol. 5, No. 3, 2004, pp97-104.

[25] Margolin, I., Pierce, J., and Wiley, A. (2011). Wellness Through a Creative Lens: Mediation and Visualization. Journal of Religion and Spirituality in Social Work: Social Thought, 2011, Vol 30, No. 3, pp234-252.

[26] Kübler-Ross, Elisabeth, David Kessler, and Maria Shriver. On Grief and Grieving: Finding the Meaning of Grief Through the Five Stages of Loss. Simon and Schuster, 2014.

[27] Imber-Black E., and Roberts J. 1992. Rituals for Our Times: Celebrating, Healing, and Changing Our Lives and Our Relationships. New York: HarperPerennial.

[28] Calhoun, Lawrence G., et al. "A Correlational Test of the Relationship Between Posttraumatic Growth, Religion, and Cognitive Processing." Journal of Traumatic Stress 13.3 (2000): 521-527.

[29] Val, E. B., & Linley, P. A. (2006). Posttraumatic Growth, Positive Changes, and Negative Changes in Madrid Residents Following the March 11, 2004, Madrid Train Bombings. Journal of Loss and Trauma, 11(5), 409-424.

[30] Calhoun, L. G., Cann, A., Tedeschi, R. G., & McMillan, J. (2000). A Correlational Test of the Relationship Between Posttraumatic Growth, Religion, and Cognitive Processing. Journal of Traumatic Stress, 13(3), 521-527.

[31] Shaw, A., Joseph, S., & Linley, P. A. (2005). Religion, Spirituality, and Posttraumatic Growth: A Systematic Review. Mental Health, Religion & Culture, 8(1), 1-11.

[32] Calhoun, Lawrence G., Richard G. Tedeschi, and Richard G. Tedeschi, eds. Facilitating PostTraumatic Growth: A Clinician's Guide. Routledge, 1999.

www.ingramcontent.com/pod-product-compliance
Lightning Source LLC
Chambersburg PA
CBHW031620040426
42452CB00007B/603